Awakening:
Catholic Women's
Ordination from the
Public Square

Myra Poole & Pippa Bonner

Fisher King Publishing

AWAKENING: CATHOLIC WOMEN'S ORDINATION
FROM THE PUBLIC SQUARE

Copyright © Myra Poole & Pippa Bonner 2015

ISBN 978-1-910406-20-5

Published by
Fisher King Publishing
The Studio
Arthington Lane
Pool-in-Wharfedale
LS21 1JZ
England

Contents

Myra Poole

Myra Poole converted to Catholicism in her early 20s, and has been a Sister of Notre Dame de Namur for nearly 60 years. She belongs to a 19th century Congregation founded in France, during the French Revolution, by St Julie Billiart, a peasant woman, with her co-founder Françoise Blin de Bourdon, a rich aristocrat.

Myra's adult religious life can be divided into two parts: the first of these being her career as a history teacher and as a Head Teacher in Northampton and Southwark, London. She then left formal education in her early 50s as she felt called to explore, with others, why women were treated like second class people in the Church. This led her to study feminist theology and spirituality in a variety of places, including Boston, USA, and to use the methodology of Titus Brandsma – TBI, Carmelite Spirituality – at Nijmegen, Holland. Her first book *Prayer, Protest, Power: The Spirituality of Julie Billiart Today* (2001) (Canterbury Press), was based on the TBI 'structural dynamic' methodology as a way to examine how she had become a Christian Feminist out of a 19th century religious charism. This was followed by *Women's Ordination: a Catalyst for Change in the Roman Catholic Church* (2003), co-written with Dorothea McEwan (Canterbury Press).

Pippa Bonner

Pippa Bonner is a wife, daughter, mother and grandmother. She recently retired from hospice work in Leeds where she ran a bereavement service. She has a social work background. She studied and obtained a theology degree when she joined Catholic Women's Ordination (CWO) 20 years ago so that she could learn more about Catholicism and feminist theology.

Pippa believes she has a calling to priestly sacramental ministry but is unable to test it out as the Roman Catholic (RC) Church does not currently help women to discern a vocation to priestly ordination. She also recognises that the outlook and structure of the Church would need to renew and reform and become less clerical, hierarchical and more inclusive and local, for women to be able to work effectively as priests within the RC Church. Pippa works as a volunteer in her parish and local hospital and is active in other renewal movements in the Church. She also writes articles of a spiritual and therapeutic nature.

Myra and Pippa have different life experiences and backgrounds. These differences are reflected in their writings but their common bond is a strong commitment, at a deeper level, to reveal the effects on women and men of the non-ordination of women.

Preface

This book was written over a period of four years. It is an attempt to write about the experience of women and men in Catholic Women's Ordination (CWO) in the Roman Catholic Church (which throughout this book will be referred to as the Catholic Church.) CWO prays and campaigns for women's ordained ministry within a reformed Catholic Church; see www.catholic-womens-ordination.org.uk

The book explores the history, theology, spirituality and emotional experience of women and men working in this and other renewal movements in the Catholic Church.

Acknowledgments

We wish to thank all those who supported us in writing this book, particularly CWO members whose experience is the fertile ground from which this book developed. Many women and men responded to questions we posed through CWO e-news, our monthly electronic Newsletter, ably edited by our Administrator Pat Brown. We asked in a small survey:

How members thought, felt and coped with the ban on women's ordination? and,

What spiritual ideas and practices kept members in CWO and if their spiritual life had grown, how had they recognised this?

This was not a scientific survey but an encouragement to members to collaborate in this book and share their experience with us.

We hope that their views have been accurately represented in this book. We recognise that some contributions have had to remain anonymous, as support for Catholic women's ordination still brings condemnation and censure from some in the Catholic Church.

We are very grateful to Pat Pinsent who read the book in its entirety and offered helpful advice and to Mary Ring for reading drafts at different stages of development and giving useful suggestions. We also thank those courageous lay people, priests, religious sisters and bishops in some parts of the world, who continue to support us, and also all those who pray that women and men will be able to use their gifts for everyone within an inclusive Church.

We dedicate this book to the many women in the world whose gifts have not been able to flourish publicly because of exclusion, poverty, and oppression imposed by others.

Catholic Women's Ordination Prayer

Moved by a compulsion of the Holy Spirit
we cannot remain ignorant
of this injustice in our midst.
We long for all humanity
to be acknowledged as equal,
particularly among your community of the church,
so we pray, grieving for the lost gifts
of so many women.

We ask you, God of all peoples,
to bring insight and integrity
to all those in positions of power,
together with an understanding that
the ascended Lord calls us all to act
doing Christ's work here and now.
We ask this of you,
God our Creator
Jesus our Redeemer
Spirit our Sustainer.

Lala Winkley

AWAKENINGS TOWARDS AN INCLUSIVE FEMINIST CATHOLIC CHURCH

Feminism

First of all we must make very clear why we have used the word 'feminist', as it is a word that is too often used in a derogatory way and totally misunderstood. The word dates from the 19th century and has been used to describe the difference between a 'patriarchal society' based on and permeated by male experience, and a 'feminist' society based on women's experience. One of the best explanations of Christian Feminism is in the following quote by Ursula King: 'Feminism is a different consciousness and vision, a radically changed perspective which calls into question many of our social, cultural, political and religious traditions ... Although it is centrally about women's experience ...feminism is therefore fundamentally about men and social change'. (King, 1989:15-22). A change of consciousness often begins with a great shock, for women as well as men, as it does not fit into the reality people inhabit. For example one young man, at a 1990s religious meeting about looking at scripture through the eyes of women, said: 'Don't bring gender into religion'! This was the beginning of an awakening, the start of a challenging journey for this man.

The development of a male Christian Feminist Theology is still in an embryonic stage. Richard Rohr, a Franciscan from the USA, is one of the few male spiritual theologians who has been concerned with the development of male spirituality. His response to this need was to set up bonding, emotional and spiritual development groups for men to explore their lives and share their experiences. A few years ago Myra was allowed to sit in on one such group, in Britain, and found it very revealing to listen to men helping each other at a deeper level. It is clear that men need many more of these groups but false male egos often stand in the way of men expressing themselves. These groups have kept very quiet and it would be helpful if the ones in Britain would gradually share some of their experiences.

Awakening

The other word that is crucial to this book is 'Awakening'. It is a long established term for spiritual experience, especially from the time of Moses. Our whole lives are filled with gradual awakenings but in times of great societal and theological shifts in understanding, they can be overwhelming as they threaten the very substance of our being. One response is to seize on these changes as life-giving ones that resonate with us; the other response, which generally predominates, is initially to resist these changes. In Church speech they are declared not to be of God, hence the persecutions of the prophets. 'Can anything good come out of Nazareth?' (Jn.1:45-46) was the first reply of Jesus's own people; to this Jesus answered 'A prophet is always without honour in their own country' (Mk. 6:4 et al.). And the most profound of all awakenings is the mystical God-given awakening in the experience of the great saints. These are the people who Evelyn Underhill calls the 'alpine climbers'[1]. Then there are most of us with our own personal insights that arise out of meditative and contemplative prayer.

Non ordination of women and violence against women

There is no greater scandal in the world of the 21st century than the growing extremes of poverty and riches. Whenever these are

---

[1] Evelyn Underhill (1875- 1914) brought mysticism from the cloister to the everyday lives of ordinary people. She was a prolific author, her best known book being *Mysticism* (1911) from which this quote is derived. She was the first woman to lecture in religion at Oxford University.

scrutinised the people at the bottom of the pile are always women and children. This book, although primarily about the position of women in the Catholic Church and specifically about women's ordination, emphasises the theoretical negative theological underpinning which is prolonging the terrible poverty of women and the violence they endure in all corners of the world.

Women's ordination only in a renewed Church

CWO differs from Roman Catholic Women Priests (RCWP)[2], who now have their own ordained women priests and Bishops. CWO decided from the beginning that was not their way to be effective. This is clearly stated in the following words of their current leaflets: *'CWO wishes to pray and campaign for women's ordained ministry within a renewed Catholic Church.'*

The Church regularly proclaims that women's ordination is not possible, and in this it is more accurate than it means to be with the current male, clerical hierarchical structures. It is not possible to develop women's ordained ministry within its present exclusive parameters. This seeking for renewal does not exclude men. In fact this theological patriarchal stranglehold is as life denying for them as it is for the many women who suffer deep oppression in this system. This is partly why so many women and men have given up on traditional organised religion. The Church has tried to keep them at the 'mythical' stage of religion, i.e. not moving beyond childhood ideas about God and Authority, even when well educated in other senses. Emotionally, they are still mythic in their religion. (See chapter

---

[2] RCWP, Roman Catholic Women Priests was founded in 2002 in Austria. The first women were ordained on the river Danube outside the restrictions of any Dioceses. They claim their ordinations are valid, through their baptisms, but illegal if judged in the context of Canon 1024. After ordination, three of the founders were ordained Bishops. This movement soon spread internationally, especially in the USA, where they are now in 32 states, and in Canada. The spread in Europe has been slower. At the moment the movement has not taken root in Britain.

6 for full explanation of this concept). This book also questions the limitations of the equality argument if it does not deepen into symbolic change. (See Chapter 5.)

Who is this book for?

This book is written for general educated readers who are looking to explore the reasons behind their own unease at the way things are at present in the Roman Catholic Church (referred to throughout the book as the Catholic Church).

This book has come about after more than twenty years of experience of CWO, especially, but not only, derived from demonstrating and praying in support of women's ordination, mainly on the Piazza of Westminster Cathedral in London during this period. Other parts of the country have held similar vigils at certain times of the year. During these past twenty years CWO has attracted members from all over the United Kingdom and other parts of the world. We have both groups and individual members from around Britain; in the early days we attracted over a hundred people to the piazza of Westminster Cathedral. As with all organisations there is a distinct difference between the first hectic 10 years and the second 10 years as the organisation went through the phase of settling in for the 'long haul'.

During the course of twenty years membership has ebbed and flowed. In spite of all this, as one antagonist said to us on the Piazza of Westminster at one of our monthly Wednesday Vigils: 'You are still here'! As circumstances change with a reforming Pope Francis, there is a renewed interest in women's ordination. Membership is gradually increasing thanks to all forms of modern media, including a CWO Facebook Page and Twitter account plus the development of our monthly CWO e-newsletter and website. Membership ages range from 25-95 so there is a vast wealth of experience among the group. The energy of this voluntary group is the binding vision to work towards a Church inclusive of all in every aspect of the Church's life.

This includes revisiting the history and present anthropology of the Church and hence the basis of some of its moral teachings.

The personal experiences on which this book is based do not constitute a quantitative sociological or scientific survey but they do reflect, in a microcosm, the greater unease in the 'macrocosm', drawing on theological and psychological thinking and a qualitative survey of CWO members' experience. Without sounding too arrogant, it is true to say that CWO has been a trail blazer, as far as women in the Church are concerned, in Britain. By its very title, CWO broke the sound barrier of silence about raising in the latter part of the 20th century the possibility of women's ordination in Britain. It initially created shock waves and recriminations from the official Church and some people called us 'the enemy within'.

The possibility of women's ordination in this Catholic tradition is gradually permeating the psyche of many in the Church. Our challenge now, with others, is to penetrate the psyche of the 'Magisterium' of the Church, (i.e. the official teaching part of the Church, the Pope and Bishops.) Pope Francis in his Apostolic Exhortation, *Evangelii Gaudium*, calls for the 'development of women's theology' but at the same time still holds on to the iconic male ideology under the term 'functional' i.e. it is necessary for priests to represent Christ in the male form.

The concept of 'Awakening' is central to the development of the argument, so each chapter of this book begins with it being applied to a different area. Awakening is a well-used spiritual term which denotes a gradual change of consciousness in both inner and outer life.

Part One: Experience

Chapter 1. Awakening to Public Action: an introduction to the origin of CWO and Women's Ordination Worldwide (WOW) and the experiences in Britain in the past 20 years. This chapter includes the monthly Wednesday prayer vigils on the Piazza of Westminster, the

Papal visit of 2010 and other personal insights on the treatment of women during this time. (Myra Poole and Pippa Bonner)

Chapter 2. Awakening from Loss Towards Resilience: an exploration of the psychological impact of being a supporter of CWO. This draws on modern loss theory, members' experiences and other sources to look at how we integrate our feelings and ways of coping with exclusion. In attempting to describe a way towards the kind of equilibrium that some members claim they need for the 'long haul', we hope to realise the degree of resilience we already have and to find some understanding of the continued emotional sustenance for the challenges ahead. (Pippa Bonner).

Chapter 3. Awakening to Spiritual Growth: an exploration that balances and feeds the campaigning energy in CWO. It looks at the work of St Teresa of Avila, Richard Rohr, Mary Grey, and Pope Francis, together with responses from CWO members and others, to encourage readers to reflect on their own spiritual ideas and experiences. (Pippa Bonner)

Part Two: History and Theology

Chapter 4: Awakening to the historically defective tradition imposed on women. This chapter uses wide historical brush strokes to trace inherited ideas about women from the Fathers of the Church to the present time. It makes the connections between this defective, culturised tradition of women with the present stance on women's non ordination and its connections with all forms of women's poverty. (Myra Poole)

Chapter 5: Awakening to 'symbolic shifts' in Feminist Theology. This includes an explanation of why the equality argument concerning the non-ordination of women is not adequate to shift the present Magisterial teaching on women. It includes a re- interpretation of the sexualised account of the Eucharist as understood by the Swiss theologian Hans Von Balthasar, re-visiting 'bride and bridegroom' symbolism, and the early thought behind the virginity of Mary and her motherhood, in the process restoring the sisterhood between Eve and Mary. The chapter ends by raising the idea of a Marian spirit filled Church: the Church of the poor. Pope Francis seems to be following this ideal, for example, by opening the Piazza in Rome to all tramps, providing public showers and haircuts on the Piazza in Rome, much to the annoyance of the rich shops nearby. (Myra Poole.)

Chapter 6: Awakening to new visions of Church: an opening up of new pathways for the re-envisioning of Church. It contains visions of future Church by various members of CWO compared with the writings of some of the leading ecclesiologists of the 20th and 21st centuries, together with a fuller development of the meaning of the mythic church and the role of individuals towards a Spirit filled Church i.e. an adult, educated church. (Myra Poole)

At the end of each chapter there are suggestions for reflection.

We hope you enjoy this book and find in it a great deal of food for further thought, discussion, disagreement but above all prayer.

Bibliography

King, Ursula (1989)*Women and Spirituality: Voices of Protest and Promise*
(New Amsterdam)
Pope Francis(2013) *Apostolic Exhortation Evengelii Gaudium (The Joy of the Gospel)*
Underhill,Evelyn (1930 12th edition) *Mysticism: A Study of the Nature of Man's Spiritual* Consciousness (E.P. Dutton)
Biblical references in Introduction, Chapters, 1,4,5,6 from New International Version, NIV (2011).

Chapter 1

AWAKENING: TO PUBLIC ACTION

'The time to assert a right is the time when that right is denied'
(Sarah Grimké 19th century reformer[3])

'Those who know they have rights must claim them' (John XXIII (1963)
Pacem in Terris.

Part One: Beginnings and first ten years

Although the quotation from Sarah Grimké was written over 200 years ago, its truth still remains today, as the twenty year experience of the CWO British Group testifies from working alongside the international group, Women's Ordination Worldwide (WOW). Most other Christian churches have now grappled with this question and have moved on to the ordination of women as priests and now as bishops. Meanwhile the Church that still calls itself the 'true Church' stumbles along screaming out with every fibre of its being that the ordination of women is a theological and scriptural impossibility. This is a Church which has forgotten its own profound scriptural belief that 'with God all things are possible' (Mt.19:26). Any reader who wants to know all the arguments for and against why women, according to the present official theology of the Church, cannot be priests will not find them here. They can be found elsewhere both on the Internet and in the books of John Wijngaards. (See bibliography and www.wijngaardsinstitute.org)

---

[3] Sarah Moore Grimké (1792-1837) was an American abolitionist, writer and member of the women's suffrage movement. Born in South Carolina to a well known plantation owner, she later moved to Philadelphia, Pennsylvania, where she became a Quaker and joined her younger sister Angelina Grimké. The sisters spoke extensively in support of the anti-slavery movement, in spite of their father's severe opposition.

We, in Women's Ordination Worldwide and in Catholic Women's Ordination have tested these arguments and found them wanting. We have been called to move to an 'awakening' that has impelled us to public action both by prayerful Vigils, especially on the Piazza of Westminster Cathedral in London, and the use of the media, radio, TV, and internet, as the only way to get an alternative voice heard. Like so many women before us we have been taken over by a power much greater than ourselves and we have been captured by a truth that will not let us go. We wish to share our story with others, and show how it has led us into a deeper understanding of the cost of following Christ.

Origins and raison d'être of CWO

2013 was the year when Catholic Women's Ordination (CWO) celebrated twenty years of its existence. During this time there have been three important high points: the origins of CWO on March 24th 1993; the first Women's Ordination Conference World Wide, (WOW) in Dublin in 2001; and the Papal visit in 2010. This chapter introduces the reader to our raison d'être and our work at raising consciousness on the crucial importance of women's ordination.

Worldwide ordination groups

Catholic Women's Ordination (CWO), like all other similar movements, arose from the margins of society and came to birth out of the circumstances of the time – in this instance, the early 1990s. Vatican II[4] (1962-1967) was succeeded by a period of ten years

---

[4] Women had been active in the early preparatory Commissions before the Vatican II, but they were not called to the Council by Paul VI until the third session. 23 women attended, including leaders of some of the Religious Congregations. The youngest was a woman of 38 from Uruguay. She was so disgusted by the way some Bishops just ignored women that she left in disgust. (See paper on Women at Vatican II on the internet *Stand up4vatican2.* and Carmel McEnroy's book entitled *Guests in Their Own House: The Women at Vatican II,* Crossroad, New York, 1996).

characterised by great hopes for change in the Church; During the 1960s, conciliar reforms, some not fully implemented, were promulgated. What is not widely known is the presence of women at Vatican II. By 1976 the hopes of growth that emerged from this Council received a great setback in the promulgation of *Inter Insigniores* (1976); Pope Paul VI declared that women could not be 'icons of Christ' i.e. priests, because they had no physical resemblance to a man. Clearly the 'icon' theory is on a very shaky theological basis as it does not take into account the whole person or the freedom of the Spirit to call whoever the Spirit chooses. Moreover it has no foundation in scripture as declared by the Scripture Commission set up by Pope Paul VI. Neither is it true that Jesus ordained men at the Last Supper. Jesus ordained no one. John Wijngaards calls this the 'Cuckoo's Egg' Tradition. (See chapter 4 below)

Women in the USA were the first to react to this declaration and were quick to respond by founding the Women's Ordination Conference, (WOC), in 1976, Canada followed in 1981 with Catholic Network for Women's Equality (CNWR). It took longer for the rest of the Catholic world to respond to the challenge but it did so in the early 1990s, which witnessed an eruption of the Spirit in Germany, Austria, Britain, Ireland, Australia and New Zealand. In Britain, CWO was formed officially in March 1993 on the Vigil of the Annunciation of Our Lady and to the surprise of us all there was a phone call from Australia to say that they too were forming a new group, which they would call Women of the New Covenant. The Holy Spirit was really working overtime! There is no doubt that all these groups were formed by the inspiration of the Spirit. Most of us had never thought we would be called to anything like this. Myra went to bed for a day when the full realisation dawned on her. Being a Religious Sister, she knew it would bring trouble to her personally. This initial fear was realised in 2001, at the first WOW Conference at Trinity College, Dublin (see below).

The Vatican's answer to this surge of the Spirit came in the Apostolic

Letter in 1994 *On Preserving Priestly Ordination to Men Alone (Ordinatio Sacerdotalis)*. This Letter came as near as it could to saying it was infallible by introducing a new theological category, using the word 'definitive'. As this new theology is very suspect the Letter will go down in history as the *"Dubious Dubium"*, as Joan Chittister OSB, liked to call it.

CWO origins and development

The origins of CWO lay in the Church of England's vote for women priests on November 11th. 1992. A few of us were in Dean's Yard, Westminster, with a large crowd, waiting expectantly for the Synod's vote. The joy on hearing it was a 'yes' vote was tangible. Many of the great pioneers were there, especially the well - known writer and activist in the Movement for the Ordination of Women (MOW), Monica Furlong, who sadly later died of cancer. When we came back for the evening's candle-lit celebrations, there was a young woman with us, Nikki Arthy, who returned with a placard, she had hastily made, saying 'Roman Catholic Women Next'. On the way home Nikki and Myra went past Archbishop's House, in Westminster. Cardinal Hume was then the Archbishop, and they posted the small placard through the Archbishop's door. Nikki has since become an Anglican priest and is very fulfilled in her calling. This was the very simple origin of CWO but the group was not formalised until the Vigil of the Annunciation on 24th March 1993. The night before, as noted above, Myra received a phone call from Australia and was told about the formation there of a similar group.

The origins of CWO were ecumenical and have remained so ever since. CWO is essentially a consciousness raising group for the sake of the whole Church. Its raison d'être is to make the connections between the non-ordination of women and women's poverty worldwide. If women are not considered 'icons of the humanity of Christ', then in their eyes and in the eyes of the world they are less human than men and therefore can be treated however any man likes: raped, kept in poverty, regarded as second class, and certainly not ordained. Women theologians have long been making the connections between the non-ordination of women and the 'sin of sexism' that runs through all aspects of the 'official' theology of the Church.

This dualistic division in the Church has been entitled 'structural sexism'. Some members of CWO do indeed feel a strong call to be women in full ministry and in all areas of the life of the Church, but all are working for deeper change in the theological understanding of 'Who and What is Church.'

The two aims of CWO are:

1) To achieve a forum for examining, challenging and developing the present understanding of priesthood.

2) To achieve the ordination of women in a renewed Church.

It is important to note that from the beginning CWO decided it would work from within the Church only and not attempt any form of ordination of its own, as has happened elsewhere.

From the start we decided to go into public places and work with the media. As women we had no other way to get our message out, as within the church we have been silenced for years on this issue and officially we are still. Our Leeds group produced a cartoon for us where we all wore a scarf around our mouths, calling it 'the no talk show'.

Our main public space from the beginning has been the Piazza of Westminster, a symbolic place, as Westminster Cathedral is the home of the Cardinals of Westminster. Without realising it, we began to find that we were reproducing some of the suffragette and suffragist tactics: the colour we chose was purple, to denote the wisdom of women and as a sign for mourning for all women's lost gifts in the Church. The importance of public vigils and the media are still the mainstay of CWO but over the years we have also honed new approaches. These include running a theological course in York for members. Some members have undertaken theological and historical education. Other reform groups, born mainly in the latter part of the twentieth century, are working towards Church renewal in various ways.

As we raised the banner for the first time, at the launch on the Piazza of Westminster on the 24th March, 1993, we all felt like suffragettes and wondered where this would take us. Lala Winkley became our creative liturgy co- ordinator, Veronica Seddon our resident artist, Peter Seddon our computer expert, Dorothea McEwan our academic, and last but not least, Ianthe Pratt our wisdom figure, who ran Lumen Women's Centre in Dulwich.   These people became the foundation group in the early years. We gained such press coverage that this alerted other parts of the country and membership increased at a rapid rate. In our early halcyon days we might get more than a 100 people joining us on the Piazza as we began our regular monthly first Wednesday Vigils. We now restrict our Vigils to certain times of the year, for example on Vocation Sunday and the feast of Mary Magdalene, the 'apostle to the apostles', and holding similar Vigils in other parts of the country.

From the beginning, CWO has held a public vigil on the Piazza of Westminster for the Chrism Mass. In most areas this takes place on the Thursday of Holy Week, but at Westminster it is held on the Tuesday. It soon became part of our tradition of peaceful vigils. The Chrism Mass is where all the priests of the Diocese are invited to celebrate their ordination. Over the years we have noticed a change of attitudes among priests: more and more have given us the thumbs up as they walk past, while others walk by with stony disapproving faces. Because of our public stance, women who did not agree with us also began to organise themselves. The two groups stood on different parts of the Piazza with different banners. Theirs usually read 'We love our priests', totally misunderstanding our message. It is very sad to meet such opposition but above all to see their influence over younger people in their midst. Nevertheless, the late Cardinal Hume, at a Diocesan meeting of priests in the early nineties, when he was asked the question, 'Could women ever be priests?' answered, 'You can never say never.'

As in most voluntary groups, the numbers in membership soon settled down and we began the hard work of the 'long haul' for change. Numbers and size are not a problem. It is an accepted norm that the raising of ideas for change is always done by the few for the sake of the many. CWO has always been blessed by a solid expanding core of very committed, tenacious group members, some who have been there from the beginning and many others who have joined along the way. In the early days London was the epicentre of most activities. Now it has spread to different parts of the country. In 2012 we began a study of Vatican II and the reforms agreed in the 1960s, and have held meetings to discuss this Council in different parts of the country during the year of faith called by Pope Benedict XVI, (2012-2013) to celebrate 50 years since the Council. These discussions have drawn in new people and increased interest.

Examples of Members' reasons for joining CWO

'What made me join CWO was seeing the pain of women who I respect greatly not being able to test their vocation.'(Catherine, Merseyside)

'Listening to women's experiences and how they had been damaged by the Institution.' (Pat, inaugural meeting of the Leeds group)

'I might have joined CWO when I was about 10 if it had been there. I argued with my father about priests being only male and got silly superficial answers about things like pregnancy (the unexpected kind) and scandal. So I was waiting ready to join.' (Cathy, Midlands.)

'From the seminary days in the fifties (in France), I have never really seen any obstacles to the ordination of women and in discussion with other dogma professors no good reasons were brought forward, and in fact some of them were as pro as I was. I think what changed for me, over the years, was the gradual realisation that women play no real part in the authority structures of the church. This sort of came to a head with the introduction of concelebration, where on diocesan occasions one would see this great phalanx of clergy gathered the other side of the "counter" with the rest of us. (I say us because I could never abide being in this clerical mass) and a majority of women, usually, the other side.' (Priest.)

'The final straw was the ordination of women in the Church of England.' (Dorothea, London.)

'I had a Damascus experience in my early 40s. I read in our diocesan newspaper that the Bishop was inviting men to consider being Permanent Deacons. I remember the unexpected pain realising I, as a woman, was not invited. I wrote and got a polite, open ended letter back. Years later when another Bishop invited the people of the diocese to go and discuss their vocations for ordination with him I wrote asking for an appointment. Many weeks later and, after the event, I got a terse letter back telling me off for asking for the opportunity. After the first occasion I saw an article in the *Guardian* in 1994 writing about the newly formed group CWO. I joined and when I received the membership directory I wrote to all the others listed in the diocese (from memory about 20 people) suggesting we meet. We held our first meeting in Leeds and a group have been meeting ever since.' (Pippa, Harrogate.)

One member recalled that CWO members are strikingly determined, brave, intelligent, welcoming and fun.

Several new members joined after reading our advertisement on London buses during the Papal visit in 2010: 'Pope Benedict Ordain Women Now.'

'The only organisation I had contact with, who were in some way acknowledging that something was amiss, and working actively to address this.' (Anon)

'I joined because of the usurpation of the feminine voice by committees of men.' (Anon)

Negative experiences from the Piazza of Westminster and elsewhere round the country

'I would rather ordain a cat than a woman.' (Echoes of sayings from the early Fathers of the church dressed up in modern guise by an Anglican priest on the verge of being received into the RC Church in 1995, Westminster Piazza.)

(The speaker had a rather prominent 'dog collar' around his neck. Myra was so angry she pulled herself up to her full height, which is nearly six foot, looked down on the young man and said 'Young man I have been a Catholic since my early twenties and a head teacher of two RC schools. How dare you speak to me like that.' He did not even go red. His arrogance was unbelievable and the leaders of the Catholic Church were preparing him for eventual priesthood in the Church!)

Questions and some responses said to CWO members

'Why do you always spoil our party?' said by a woman on the occasion of the ordination of three Church of England Bishops to the 'Ordinariate' in 2011.

'Women can never be ordained because they are not capable of being priests' is often said and always accompanied by looks of horror that we dare to stand there with banners saying 'Where are our women priests?' or 'Catholic Women's Ordination'.

On one occasion a woman was so angry with us she tried to take our banner and said, 'why are you still here?' (This was after we had been at least ten years on the Piazza).

'Must do what the Pope says' was said, and illustrates the devastating damage that 'patriarchal hierarchical theology' has done to so many

RC members: 'the Pope has spoken' marks the end of all discussion, exemplifying the 'Father says' tradition. (Piazza)

It is also clear that many cultural myths are still deeply embedded in the minds of so many people. For example the question of the 'blood taboos' has still not been eradicated from all religions. It was not understood why women menstruated, so they were considered inferior and the mystery (and even the alleged magic) of women bleeding regularly frightened people. Scientific evidence on male semen was only discovered in the 19th century with the invention of the microscope. It took till the early 20th century for the beginning of an understanding about monthly periods not being 'unclean' or a 'curse', but a part of the richness of women's nature for the whole of creation[5].

A group held a women's ordination vigil as an Anglican priest was being received into the Church in Caerphilly. Nearly everyone was positive except for one very agitated woman who said loudly, 'menstruation on the altar!' This sentiment was repeated yet again on another occasion: 'Women cannot be priests because they menstruate' – modern echoes of the blood taboos of past ages.

Over the years we have noticed a variety of responses to our cause ranging from total support to vile abuse and the frightening arrogance of certainty from priests as well as from lay people. This was particularly marked on the occasion of the consecration of the Ordinariate Bishops in 2011. A group of seminarians from London were walking into Westminster Cathedral, when they saw our banner; only one dared come and talk to us – The rest were clearly

---

[5] *Blood Taboos* (Ecumenical Forum of European Christian Women by the Commission on Theology and Spirituality, 1990-1994.

scared. The lecturer who was accompanying them turned on us in a superior and almost pitiful way saying that what we asked was impossible and we were wasting our time. Fortunately we are so sure of our ground that we are sorry for those whose minds have been so closed by their very training to the priesthood. Many have nicknamed the Ordinariate as the 'youcominism', as the then Vatican thinking on ecumenism.

Are women more negative than men?

Mixed responses came from this question depending on the depth of reaction

'Yes, standing outside St Anne's Cathedral, Leeds and outside Westminster Abbey some years ago it was women who came up and shouted, their faces turning red with anger, right in our faces'.

'Outside Westminster Cathedral during the Papal visit of 2012, a priest accompanied by two younger priests looked at the banner and said "Why don't you join the Church of England?"'

The next two remarks sum up the present situation clearly:

'I find that there is no set rule to this, and that women, irrespective of class etc. can have very different views. However, those who have been culturised to lean towards male leadership are very cautious of upsetting the status quo and see questioning male leadership as questioning God. I also find that women who have a reasonable understanding of history of the Church are more likely to have the skills to question the status quo.' (Scotland).

'It seems to me that the anger shown by men is different from the anger shown by women: men are angry because their status is being questioned i.e. their rightful leadership power because of their sex. This may well be your alpha male or one who is very unsure of who he is.' (Scotland).

Positive experiences

Some people have been very complimentary and said, 'it is about time this happened.' This is especially notable from people who come from Europe.

Some priests say, 'Keep it up – we can't do it.'

'No reason women cannot do what men do.'

'It is about time this happened in the Church.'

'It is a scandal it has not happened yet.'

'What age does the Vatican live in? – the dark ages?'

Several members commented that it is no doubt easier to stand in a place where you are not known than doing so locally at one's own Cathedral.

Erosion of trust

All members were scandalised by the worldwide paedophilia Church scandal and this quote from a CWO member sums up the seriousness of the scandal: 'A scandal that is far more serious in a Church that calls itself Christian than in secular society. People's trust has been deeply eroded putting all hierarchical authority at risk of tumbling into a pit. It has left very deep marks of no credibility in many minds, both said and unsaid.'

Women's Ordination Worldwide Dublin 2001:
the emergence of public Magisterium opposition

(The Magisterium, as mentioned, is the teaching authority of the RC Church, vested currently in the Pope with his Bishops.)

Women's Ordination Worldwide (WOW) was born, in an Upper Room with 72 Catholics present, at the First Women's Synod held in Austria in 1996. The name was chosen unanimously by those present. Since then it has become the international arm of the whole movement. The first conference was to be in Dublin in 2001. Dublin was chosen because it was in a very well -known Catholic country that has given so many missionaries to countries all over the world. The Irish group, the 'Brothers and Sisters in Christ', agreed to host the conference and a working group was formed.

From the beginning it was very controversial. The then Archbishop of Dublin heard of it and so began major opposition. In order to prevent church interference the organisers had to choose a non- catholic venue – University College Dublin. The speakers were agreed early on as including Aruna Gnandason, from the women's desk of the World Council of Churches, (WCC); Joan Chittister OSB, the well-known Benedictine speaker from Eyrie, USA; and John Wijngaards, now of the Wijngaards Institute in London, who has done so much academic work on the internet to inform the world on all the arguments for and against women priests and whose work has been translated into many languages.

Myra Poole was the co-ordinator of WOW at this time. As the time of the conference drew nearer, 'little letters', as Joan Chittister loved to call them began to appear. Firstly a letter was sent to the then President of the World Council of Churches in Geneva, to say that Aruna, the ecumenical representative from the Council, was requested to withdraw from the conference. After much soul searching for ecumenical relationships, Aruna decided not to come to the conference but she sent a copy of her paper to be read by all.

President Raiser, however, was then asked to rescind the £1,000 donation given by the Council to WOW. He declined and said financial matters were a matter for the Council. The Catholic Church is not an official member of the WCC and therefore had no say in this area. Then came an email to Myra from Joan Chittister OSB, saying she had received a letter. (At this stage Myra had no knowledge of such a letter having also be sent to her own Superior; the latter was away visiting sisters overseas and wisely did not raise the issue till her return.)

Joan's Prioress, Christine Vladimiroff, did all she could to allay Vatican fears, even going to Rome to give them the subject and contents of Joan's speech, entitled 'Discipleship for a Priestly People in a Priestly Age'. But nothing could pacify Rome. Myra's Superior meanwhile returned to London and she was told she also had a 'little letter', in Joan Chittister's phrase. These 'little letters' grew to three in number, each one more and more demanding. In the end Joan was able to get the support of all her Sisters since she lived in community with them all. Myra's situation was different as she belonged to a worldwide order so that the effect on the sisters in developing countries had to be considered. Their difficult situations of poverty and cultural trends were and still are very different from those of us who live in the West. The Superiors of both orders had been charged by the Vatican to put Joan and Myra under obedience not to go. The implication was that if we did go we would have to leave our Congregations. Myra was advised by her Superior not to go and was asked to think about it. After a fortnight of sheer torture Myra decided she had to go especially to warn the Religious who were coming from Asia and Africa.

In much trepidation Myra went to Dublin and to the Conference and said she had never been so terrified in her life as she thought the result of her action would give her Superiors no choice but to dismiss her from the Congregation. The press took these stories up in force and came out in full support of Joan and Myra. The internet and emails poured in to the Vatican supporting them, including Religious Congregations who stopped their meetings and came out in support. The developing countries did likewise. Myra received over 1,000 emails on her part, while Joan, who was much better known, must have had many more. Myra's are now safely kept in the Women's Library at the London School of Economics. The result of this solidarity was that Rome had to climb down, not by sending a personal letter to the Superiors of the Orders, but by a Press Release. Today it would be put on 'Twitter' and Facebook! The then Pope's press spokesperson Joaquin-Navarro – Vallis wrote: 'While the Congregation for the Institutes of Consecrated Religious had thought "the Sisters' participation inopportune" because of the possibility of outside manipulation, the Congregation never considered taking disciplinary measures.'

A full account of this situation can be read in *Making All Things New: women's ordination in the Catholic Church – a catalyst for change* (2002, chapter 5) by Dorothea McEwan and Myra Poole. This event and responses to this event are an important part of the process of 'awakening', not only for Aruna, Joan and Myra but for the whole of CWO and WOW. They proved so clearly the depth of fear that pervaded the Vatican, especially the Curia, at that time. This incident is a clear example of the 'Blue Print' fossilised ecclesiology (explained and discussed in Chapter 6) as it shows up the short comings of the papacy that tries to govern by threats and fear by silencing all legitimate opposition. The irony is if they had not raised such a controversy about the Conference, the press would not have been so interested. As a result of their actions this Conference gained worldwide coverage and publicity, such is the way the Holy Spirit works: The God of the 'back door' as Edwina Gateley, (the founder of the Voluntary Missionary Movement in 1969) would say.

Media

From the beginning there was intense media presence with the launch of CWO as the Anglican Church began its preparations for ordaining its first women priests. CWO launched with a press conference, such was the interest. Nikki Arthy, one of the younger members, now an Anglican priest, was photographed carrying an enormous banner saying 'HOPE FOR WOMEN PRIESTS'. The group asked Myra to co-ordinate the press, and as a result, many members who were willing found themselves in radio stations to answer questions on the attitude of the 'official' RC Church towards this question. In the first three months Myra was besieged by the media, a situation which continued for at least ten years. Now times are changing: some members have had media training and many have gradually found the confidence to speak out in public on this important issue. The result is that a richness of experience has emerged in different parts of Britain as the following examples illustrate.

Part 2: The second ten years (Pippa Bonner – Leeds group)

In 2005 the Leeds CWO Group had finished organising a two year course in York on liturgical and pastoral studies, to complement academic theological education. The course was open to lay women and men. The participants came from around the country. Course companions (tutors) and assignments were offered. It was recognised that the ethos of the course was not hierarchical. Experienced contributors gave their time over the two years. When this course finished a number of those who had been involved gathered again in York to contribute to a Channel 4 programme with Christina Odone.

We gathered with her in a circle, held a simple liturgy and contributed our experiences in a discussion with her. She cried in one instance, while the camera men were visibly moved by the stories. Some of the contributors told of pain, persistence, discrimination and struggle in trying to engage with the clerical hierarchy about discerning and testing the priestly vocation, to which some women felt the call by the Holy Spirit. These women were, and are, unable to test a calling and are (still) forbidden from discussing it within the Church, since the Pope's definitive statement in 1994. (*Ordinatio*

Sacerdotales) Christina concluded our part of the programme by saying that she had feared CWO was damaging the Church but had now realised how much the Church had damaged the lives of the women she had met. Her views may have changed since but on that afternoon in York those there felt we had engaged with her and each other in effective dialogue.

The Papal visit 2010

This was the other highlight of the first twenty years and what a success it was! It drew in, not only our own members, who came from all over the country, but also people from many other groups.

By 2010 CWO had decided to speak out publicly to the media about women's ordination during the Pope's visit to the UK if given the opportunity. To this end some CWO members did some media training.

In preparing for the Pope's visit, the decision to pay for 30 London buses to advertise this statement 'Pope Benedict Ordain Women Now' was made (and paid for with a legacy left to CWO.) The fact that this was carried out was thanks to the work of our administrator, Pat Brown, from Leeds, who took to this task with great gusto. Low and behold the advertisement was to be on the buses for a month! During the Papal visit these buses were proudly going around London with this very clear message on their side. The strapline was devised by Cathie, one of our north-west members.

Nobody foresaw how this would start intense media interest. The CWO mobile did not stop ringing and soon some members were doing radio and TV interviews in the studio in London, the north of England and elsewhere. CWO Members (and some of us also spoke for a sister group Catholic Voices for Reform) were being interviewed on BBC News and on BBC radio religious programmes around the UK in the days before Pope Benedict arrived in the UK. Media from around the world filmed some CWO members holding a prayer vigil on the Westminster Piazza on the eve of the Pope's visit to England.

The BBC News cameras and other stations followed a CWO procession from Southwark to Lambeth, the CWO presence outside Lambeth Palace, Hyde Park and in Birmingham outside Oscott College. Peter Tatchell, the gay activist, came to support us because of the discrimination women are experiencing in the Roman Catholic Church. He directed all media enquiries to CWO members around him. After some live coverage of the Lambeth procession and its immediate aftermath appeared, no further material was broadcast, although UK media cameras were filming. CWO concluded that the UK media were being censored somewhere: there is some oral evidence of this happening. Reports continued to appear in the written press, namely *The Times* and *Guardian*.

Film crews from Reuters, the U.S. Canada, Russia, France, Italy and many other countries continued to interview CWO members about women's ordination and the Pope's visit.

Members have subsequently developed in confidence and regularly write to *The Tablet* and other papers. Facebook, Twitter and Blogs are other useful ways to spread the word and widen the interest of women and men in different countries, especially those of younger age groups. CWO has become 'savvy' in seizing opportunities to put the CWO perspective forward, locally and nationally.

Conclusion

This experience from our vigils in public spaces highlights the fierce opposition that those who dare to question Rome have to be willing to experience for the sake of the cause.

Many have already trodden this path of being silenced or castigated, women as well as men, but mainly theologians and Religious, because as a result of their public vows the Magisterium of the Church has much more control over them. This is clearly illustrated in *From Inquisition to Freedom* by the Australian Paul Collins (2001), which tells the stories of seven prominent Catholics and their struggle with the Vatican; the stories include those of   Charles

Curran, an American moral theologian; Tissa Balasuriya OMI a Sri Lankan theologian, censured for his views on other religions, named as 'relativism'; Jeannine Gramick and Robert Nugent, for their work with the gay community; Lavinia Byrne for her book *Women at the Altar* which was burned by the Liturgical Press in the USA; Hans Kung for his critique of Papal Infallibility; and the author himself, Paul Collins. But there are many more, unknown, who have suffered severely at the hands of Rome, a phenomenon sometimes referred to as the 'modern inquisition'.

The changing arguments re women and priesthood have altered over the ages. At the moment in the Church we are moving from the 'icon argument' of Pope Paul VI in 1976 in *Inter Insigniores,* to 'the Church has no authority argument' of John Paul II. Pope Francis currently says the door is closed to women's ordination. He understands the all-male priesthood as 'functional'. (Chapter 4 explains these historical twists and turns and terms.)

Reflections

- Consider insights that have come to you through this chapter
- How do they resonate with your own experience?
- Reflect on your reactions and why.

Bibliography

Ecumenical Forum of European Christian Women by the Commission on Theology and Spirituality,1990-1994. *Blood Taboos*

Byrne,Lavinia (1999) *Women at the Altar* (Continuum publishing, New York).

Collins. Paul (2001) *From Inquisition to Freedom: Seven Prominent Catholics and their Struggle with the Vatican* (Simon and Schuster, Australia).

Mc Enroy,Carmel (1996) *Guests in their own House, the Women of Vatican II* (Crossroads, New York.)

McEwan. Dorothea, Ed.,(1991) *Women Experiencing Church: A Documentation of Alienation* (Gracewing, Fowler Wright Books, Leominster, Hertfordshire).

McEwan. Dorothea and Poole, Myra (2002) *Making All Things New: Women's Ordination in the Catholic Church – a catalyst for change* (Canterbury Press, Norwich)

Chapter 2
AWAKENING:
FROM LOSS TOWARDS RESILIENCE

'No journey into change is easy. It is fraught with pitfalls,
pain and joy'. (Ann, CWO)

'It was a shock to go public and listen to people's insults in London
and Leeds when we stood outside our Cathedrals. My calling to
ordained ministry, first heard twenty years ago has not gone away,
despite silence or dismissal from many in authority in the church. My
sadness and anger has now mostly been channelled into keeping
going, deeper conviction, and companionship with others along the
road. Part of me, continuing this path, has encountered loss, and
dying to what might have been. I know there is more suffering ahead,
but it is combined with joy and confident hope.' (Pippa, CWO)

This chapter is written for CWO supporters and many others working
for renewal, who believe that some of the practices, liturgies and
outlook for women in the modern Catholic Church are limited, and
are convinced that women are called to take a more active role. Lay
men too often feel their gifts are not used to the full. We read in the
Gospels of how Christ worked with women – Martha and Mary, Mary
Magdalene and many others. Women's role in the Early Church is
written about frequently in the Epistles, examples being Phoebe in
Paul's letter to the Romans 16.1-3 and the women in 1 Tim.3:8-12, (See
wijngaardsinstitute.org for historical and biblical references to
women working as deaconesses, leaders, teachers, prophets and
more in the Early Church.) Elisabeth Schüssler Fiorenza has written
about equal discipleship (1986).

What is the connection between the last chapter, about the
beginnings of CWO and awakening to public action, and this chapter

about the concept of loss, and even a kind of 'dying', like the seed? 'Unless a wheat grain falls on the ground and dies, it remains only a single grain; but if it dies, it yields a rich harvest.' (Jn.12:24)

For many of us in reform groups, awakening to ideas of renewal, and taking public action, can be a shock. Our composure can be shaken. Change can be threatening but it may be an exciting opportunity! Discovering that we are called to speak out may be an exciting challenge for some while for others it is frightening. Realising we are being silenced, especially if we experience a calling to ordained ministry and renewal, can seem like a loss or a 'dead end' if the way forward is barred and we are not allowed to test out the call, or as a reformer, to move forward. Loss may include a lack of understanding from others, and even threats and censure, along with rejection of what we believe, are God-given gifts. We each find a way of dealing with this awakening but it is likely to involve a period of grieving, dying to oneself and our existing way of life, before discerning a way to God in a different and perhaps more meaningful and increasingly resilient manner. We look at developing and deepening spirituality in Chapter 3. Chapter 2 is concerned with some of the psychological and emotional impact we may have to work through to learn to cope with change and renewal.

Coping with loss and change

Firstly, CWO members and non members replied to questions I posed and some of their answers are used throughout the chapter to show how they think, feel and respond. [6] The emotional long term impact that an unrecognised calling to priestly vocation, and the effect that

---

[6] The personal quotations in this chapter come from members and non-members of CWO. Some responded to questions I asked, about how they felt and coped with the ban on women's ordination in the Roman Catholic Church. The questions were asked in CWO eNews, a monthly e communication sent by CWO Administrator Pat Brown to CWO members (unedited) and non members (edited).

the struggle with male clerical hierarchical structures can have on members, and other people seeking renewal in the Church, are illustrated throughout this chapter.

Secondly, the chapter includes consideration of a theoretical model of Loss (Stroebe and Schut, 2001), which is used globally in relation to loss, bereavement and change. This is shown to be applicable to everyone.

Thirdly there is a discussion of how women and men in CWO, and others seeking renewal, may develop resilience out of their experience, to enable them to journey towards a healthy integration of feeling, thought and action to support them in a process of change. This includes discernment and the channelling of emotions and experiences in different ways.

Many of us have been disappointed by structural obstacles placed by the Church when we try to be true to our faith journey. Here two women describe different aspects of the loss they experience:

'Christian anger is a God given gift, a spur to make things better for all, not just for ourselves. When this anger is harnessed to work with other people for change, it becomes a very powerful weapon fuelled by the Spirit. It enables us to work for the 'long haul', with patience, knowing this is God's work, not ours, and allowing ourselves to be led by the Spirit in all we do. No journey into change is easy. It is fraught with pitfalls, pain and joy.' (Ann, CWO)

'As a woman experiencing the call to ordained ministry in the Roman Catholic Church, I think it's true to say that every aspect of my being has been in some way truncated by the bar to a full living out of this calling in my prayer community. Perhaps "wounded" would be a better metaphor so as to convey the pervasive sense of injury and pain ... However, I'm increasingly certain that being in a position to let wound speak to wound in prayer does constitute a living out of Christian ministry that can open space for God's gift of resurrection.' (Olive, CWO)

Ann and Olive describe different ways of coping with loss and the emotions it engenders. Olive alludes to the pervasive effect on her life of being barred from living out her vocation. She then describes how she coped with that in a way that is leading to personal and spiritual recovery and growth for her self and others. Ann speaks of grief and anger that she has channelled into a more positive and joyful place. If we are persistently knocking at a closed door and our calling is continually ignored, rejected or ridiculed, how does that make us feel and act? Is there an opportunity for positive growth developing from this place on the doorstep?

I worked in a hospice for 23 years with dying people, their families and friends, and ran a bereavement service. I was working with people who were grieving a death. Often they discussed other major losses and events in their lives which compounded their grief: rejection, illness, unemployment, divorce, abuse, and other major traumas and life transitions which they needed to mourn and work through.

It seems to me that women and men experiencing long term rejection of their gifts or vocation, those living with 'what might have been or what might be', unable to test out a priestly vocation that they see as part of their core identity, together with those subject to ridicule for supporting women's ordained ministry, are all coping with a living loss. They are grieving for this loss, just as in other forms of bereavement. It might be helpful to try and apply a current loss and grief model to the living loss of being denied priestly ministry and other opportunities to offer our gifts, and see if it might assist us to cope for the 'long haul', while we continue to pray and campaign in renewal groups. Other members agree that a mourning or adaptive process is needed to work through the potential damage which this loss, if left unattended, can bring in the long term. It is not suggested that members and reformers necessarily need grief counselling, but rather that a healthy self-awareness of loss and working through it individually, might assist us to move forward with greater strength towards our personal and group life goals. Personal self awareness and development sits alongside spiritual growth and an increased awareness, explored in Chapter 3.

Stroebe and Schut's *Dual Process Model of Coping with Grief* (1999, 2001.)

The Stroebe and Schut Model was developed from research looking originally at male and female coping styles in bereavement. This Model is now used globally with bereaved people, and those facing other losses such as unemployment, discrimination, long term illness, or other major living loss. It recognises individual styles of coping with loss. I consider it is a collaborative, empowering Model which grieving people can use and work out their own way forward, if they wish. It seems to me from applying it extensively in my past hospice work with people, and receiving feedback from them, that it accommodates cultural, gender and age differences and is 'user friendly'.

Stroebe and Schut 2001

A Dual Process Model of Coping with Grief
Loss-orientated   Restoration- orientated

❖ grief work
❖ facing grief
  breaking bonds/ties
❖ intrusion of grief
❖ denial/avoidance of
  restoration changes

❖ attending to life
  changes
❖ doing new things
❖ distraction from grief
❖ denial/avoidance of
  grief
❖ new roles identities
  relationships

Oscillation

Everyday life experience

Loss Oriented Side of the Dual Process Model

On the *Loss orientated side* people tend to respond to grief by trying to face the emotions of grief, the sadness, anger and guilt and acknowledging that the person (or what is now no longer there) is not physically present in the same way. I believe this can apply to a life goal that is being blocked. The survivor's original life plan is no longer seemingly possible. The 'breaking bonds and ties' does not mean forgetting those who have died (or a life goal) but finding a different way of connecting with them/it, for instance through memories, love and hope of finding a different way forward. The 'intrusion' of grief mentioned is like the tidal wave of emotion that can come unexpectedly and be transiently overwhelming. Some people resist or delay the long term processing of their grief and the working through of some of the acute emotional pain. The Loss Mode has been seen as the so called 'female' way of coping with grief, although many men recognise that this is also their predominant way of thinking and feeling after a major loss. (The original research for this model was done with older bereaved people whose partner had died.) Younger people now, in my professional experience, seem to exhibit mixtures of so called 'male' and 'female' ways of thinking and feeling. These can be dependent on socialisation, cultural norms and individual development.

M, C, S and J in CWO all speak of how alone they felt as children or young women discussing a sense of calling or aspiration with those around them who did not hold similar views. Feelings of isolation, anger and being 'fobbed off' were experienced by these women when younger. This compounded their grief. Rachel says 'I have found actively protesting & challenging the status quo in a direct way is not helpful to me – I get too angry!' One CWO group said: 'Rage can be a positive emotion if channelled wisely at times, whereas at other times resignation and patience is useful.' Another woman in a group described 'clinging by my finger-nails' to the Church, after many years of being a CWO member. M said some of her relatives doubted her sanity when she spoke of women's ordination. Pat was told by strangers 'You'll burn in hell.' How would that make any of us feel?

The wearing of purple by CWO members, considered by some as a colour of mourning, may link with the Loss Mode. Some think it important to focus on the difficult struggle, as they see it, and the sufferings that the hierarchical Church, from which they are excluded, inflicts on them. They talk of the anger, the sadness they feel and they find ways to live with alienation and exclusion, perhaps in a place of struggle; this then is a valid, authentic place for them. Members may feel supported, but the cohesive energy may come from a common sense of the pain they feel together.

Restoration Oriented Side of the Dual Process Model

The *Restoration side of the Dual Process Model* is no 'better' or 'worse' than the Loss mode but it is a different response to the loss. It was seen as the so-called 'male' way of coping with grief, but many women recognise that they think and feel predominantly this way. It acknowledges that there is grief and finds ways to deal with it by attending to the life changes that this bereavement or loss brings. It allows a certain degree of avoidance and distraction so that work and other tasks can be undertaken, and this distraction, in moderation, is seen to be 'healthy' or 'normal.' Otherwise how would we parent our children, drive a car or work safely and continue to engage with life while grieving acutely?

How can we pick up and engage with life if women's inclusion in ordained ministry is denied? Many CWO members report that campaigning, developing inclusive liturgies and empowering others in the UK and the developing world are all ways of managing their loss. Rachel says 'The only way I have found of coping with the current situation is ... in my prayers – both public (e.g. at Mass) or private (e.g. reading a spiritual book), I constantly use/mentally translate phrases into a less sexist language – I always read 'He' and 'Lord' (referring to

Mother Father) as 'God'. In casual conversations about priesthood I will use the pronouns he and she, refer to women and men etc. as if this were already the norm ... This way is more subversive, unsettles and raises eyebrows, and (I hope) quietly whittles away at attitudes which are born from common practice and habit.'

Two group responses describe how they manage without an apparent immediate hope of change: "Here I stand I can do no other" – Martin Luther's call resonates today and is what we feel to be our motivating belief – to keep on going even when it all seems pretty dire'; and 'Our loyalty to the Church requires us to carry on – it would be too easy to walk away (which is what so many others have done in despair).' Another member comforts herself with the notion that 'The suffragettes might have lost hope at times but they didn't give up'

Sue says how she copes: 'Mostly I try to go to meditation groups, but I also go to Mass in my own church where there is a strong feeling of community.' Pippa finds 'daily Mass in a parish community with a collaborative priest sustaining, and a place of balance in the day. I also am a member of a hospital chaplaincy team where I can use some of my pastoral gifts.' Sue also copes with a focus: 'One of the main reasons for the struggle is to reach out to women in the two-thirds of the world who so often suffer just for being women and whose bodies men so often abuse.' A CWO group said they tried to deal with their feelings of loss with an aim: 'We felt that our emotions were tied up with the issue of justice and equality – giving us a focus for our emotions.' Solidarity with the CWO movement – locally, nationally and internationally – mutual encouragement, support and sharing of ideas and ways of promoting the campaign are important. 'We don't feel we have a choice but to continue on – now we have started on the journey – something has to change and we wish to be part of it.' Obstinacy and 'pig-headedness' were also mentioned as coping mechanisms.

When asked what supports them those questioned often acknowledged the Sacraments, especially The Eucharist, but seldom mentioned anything else church-based, especially with the introduction of the new liturgy. Many members said prayer as well as the sacraments sustained them. Some also noted that CWO liturgies in particular were a source of strength. One said, 'The strategy I have for keeping going is to participate in women's liturgies of various sorts, where we take it in turn to lead. I also try to develop myself theologically and see where the Spirit is leading.' One of our founder members, Lala, has always seen that creating liturgies on the Westminster Cathedral Piazza or at CWO gatherings has been key in sustaining and empowering CWO members to pray, come together and support each other spiritually.[7]

For many, being together in groups is important. In the Restoration Mode a group may acknowledge their pain but focus more on how they will cope with the outcome rather than on the process: 'Come and join CWO and be sustained by the companionship in the common struggle that it may offer!' Members have fun together too and most recognise that they have to have a sense of humour to survive. In the Restoration Mode members may be wearing purple, not so much as a mourning colour but because from baptism purple signifies dignity, priesthood and royalty. And they may also concentrate on the belief that they are aligned with others who are excluded, for example: the poor, the women in the developing world, and the Lesbian, Gay, Bisexual and Transgender (LGBT) Movement, who are regarded by many as being excluded from orthodox, conservative Catholicism. Restoration energy perhaps comes from working for future renewal and inclusion.

Oscillation

The oscillation between these two modes (Loss and Restoration) is the important dynamic in this Model. Grief is often described as a 'rollercoaster' experience, as people oscillate back and forth and up

---

[7] See Bibliography for books about liturgy, though the list is far from being comprehensive.

and down between these two modes. At an acute phase, some will move between them several times a day. Others will get stuck in one mode. Staying consistently in the Loss mode might lead to clinical depression or anxiety, while being 'stuck' in the Restoration mode (perhaps easier in our modern western 24/7 society which exhorts: 'work hard, play hard, and be constantly diverted') might lead to a sustained avoidance of grief and a manic busy-ness. Delayed grief might emerge very acutely some time after the event.

In CWO I have come to recognise this rollercoaster dynamic. For periods of time we grieve for what might have been and at other times we work for women's ordination in the future. Our liturgies reflect this oscillation between reflecting on intense internal loss and external future mission. Working and praying in groups helps us to support each other. The Pope's Visit to the U.K. in 2010 when we came together to walk and pray was a high point for many of us. The media wanted to speak to us. We responsibly gave voice on television, radio and in print to how we felt and how we worked for women's ordination. The CWO poster printed on thirty London buses that said 'Pope Benedict Ordain Women Now!' attracted a lot of attention. It was a real boost to see some of those buses stuck in traffic giving many bystanders time to read the message. Then we would recall that back in our parishes, official discussion was 'forbidden.' Thus it was indeed a rollercoaster ride ...

I have found the Stroebe and Schut Model to be very collaborative. I present the diagram to many grieving people with whom I am working, including those experiencing other losses, and *they* decide the Mode where they predominantly are, or where is their 'comfort zone'. Then I ask them to consider if they need to move to the other mode more of the time, and how they do that and grieve 'healthily' in a way they can manage. I have worked using the Model with couples who say they can't talk to each other about this bereavement or loss, or that one of them doesn't seem to be grieving. This Model may help them to see that the other family member may be grieving just as much as they are, but behaving differently. It is useful for members to consider this in their renewal groups. By working on their shared experience they can develop a new spiritual identity and a stronger spirituality.

Oscillation is the point of resilience

Mention is made frequently in the world of grief about the concept of resilience in bereavement or loss. This is often cited in relation to how children are coping with grief, with school, or with life in general, as well as with adults. In this Model, *the oscillation is perceived as the point of resilience*, rather than either of the Loss or Restoration Modes as such (cf. Relf, Machin and Archer 2008.) Resilience in this context is defined as not being potentially either overwhelmed in the Loss mode or over controlling or managing in the Restoration mode. Instead what is needed is the capacity to hold, at the same time, both the pain *and* the growth and ability to attend to life's tasks. This resilience becomes a point of new balance or equilibrium, derived from our own experience.

I have also presented this Model at a CWO retreat. Members worked out where they were within the Model and reflected on their grief about the Church not accepting their gifts or vocation, together with what they needed to do to continue working for renewal in a way that was sustainable. Individuals and groups can also oscillate. Sometimes people may feel hopeful and engaged with renewal and/or their own lives, and at other times frustrated, withdrawn and disheartened. It is important to recognise that individuals have different past life experiences which they bring with them. These experiences may make them more fragile or stronger for the work to be done. Some groups will bond because they are responding to a common external issue. Others may fragment because external or internal pressures are too strong. Any individual's interaction with a group will impact both on themselves and on the whole group. Allowing time to build up a group will help to strengthen many, but not all, groups. Not all people work well in groups. Differences need to be respected.

Resilience in CWO and other renewal groups

How might the features of oscillation and resilience be present in CWO and other renewal groups? Some of us recognise that we can feel sad *and* continue to work for change. The capacity to hold both loss and restoration at the same time also involves paradox and an acceptance of the place of uncertainty, rather than a fixation on polarised thinking (either/ or options) and the need for certainty and structure. I believe this capacity to hold the pain and the on-going activities of life is linked to our spiritual lives, and our development and maturation, something which is reflected in the life and work of such notable figures as Joan Chittister, Mary Grey, Joyce Rupp, Richard Rohr, Daniel O'Leary and others. (See bibliographies of Chapters 2 and 3). Some of us in the Roman Catholic Church have grown up with an over-reliance on being told what to do, and a need for certainties and structure. We may be prone to a more rigid way of thinking that requires us to obey the rules and demands total obedience, rather than permitting questioning, and a reliance on personal conscience or initiative. Other people may be able to live with the uncertainties, the questions, the paradox, and thus to feel free to explore and to believe in the appropriateness of going in the more prophetic, contemplative, uncharted directions that present themselves to us. The resilient, oscillating place is where this balance might be maintained – in the sadness *and* the hope, the certainties *and* the uncertainties, in the orthodoxy *and* the new visions of church. This is perhaps the place of growth.

If we can hold both the pain and the forward focus CWO can become a place of strength, a well from which to draw sustenance. Similarly, as people recognise the shift between the two modes in themselves and in each other, they can recognise that both ways of expressing grief, loss and change are valid and to be respected. Cathy says 'I have passed through stages such as anger or impatience. For me now, the most effective objective is to maintain a confident, compassionate stance of opposition to discrimination and to engage support whenever possible. Being in CWO, as well as in related or similar women's groups, is what makes this effort possible.' Members can support each other through the ups and downs. The 'outside', the 'edge' becomes the new centre, the new equilibrium, the new place from which to work for women's ordained ministry.

An example of the 'outside' becoming the new 'centre'.

I recall Victoria, an American Roman Catholic Woman Priest, (RCWP) (see explanation for the differences between CWO and RCWP in the Introduction) telling me that gay people were excluded from Mass in a large US Cathedral. She and others started to say Mass in the street outside for those barred from the building at Mass times. Every weekend more people started to attend the street Mass, so that these Masses became powerful celebratory welcoming signs of real faith. After a number of weeks, many of those inside the Cathedral came to join those outside in the cold of winter. The grief and sense of isolation of those who had been excluded from Mass was recognised (Loss mode) and a creative solution was put in place (Restoration mode), both being held together in a new equilibrium which gathered strength and empowered everyone in it who felt in pain and excluded. The result seemed more powerful than the starting point. No doubt, people oscillated between sadness and going forward and back during this process. Exclusion was not being denied. The outcome was more powerful than if the excluded group had been taken into a private place somewhere for a joint liturgy. If only all Catholic communities would follow this example of working with the excluded!

The combination of both inclusion and shared liturgy in such a public space led to a new empowerment for the once excluded individuals and the once included group. For them, initially, the street was the only place, and it subsequently became the preferred place to be, despite the cold weather. It is the place where Christ is found in the 'last will be first', upside down, non-hierarchical community he envisaged for his Church. In the words of the *Magnificat*, (Lk.1:46-55): 'He has pulled down princes from their thrones and exalted the lowly. The hungry he has filled with good things, the rich he sent empty away.'

An institutional example of grief being avoided and displaced.

Aspects of the Paedophilia Crisis illustrate this point. In contrast to the above, using this same model of loss, this institutional example shows how immersed the Church – supposedly immune to self-examination – has become.

What about when grief is avoided or displaced on to others? What may happen when it is the institutional Catholic Church which may be guilty of this? The psychologist Mary Frawley - O'Dea (2012, *National Catholic Reporter*) makes the interesting observation that, following the exposure of the clerical sexual abuse scandal, she believes the Church hierarchy (at the time of her article in 2012) had been unable to mourn the loss of how the Church used to be perceived. It now had a flawed reputation and had lost some influential power following the cover up that was currently being revealed. (This was of course in addition to the loss of children's innocence and the terrible damage done to those abused.)

She wrote from the American perspective and focused on how the American religious sisters and some priests had exhorted the Catholic community to look at this suffering. They began to insist that priestly ministry be expanded to include women and married men. She wrote that, on the whole at that moment, the Church was 'unable to respond adaptively to ... loss through a process of healthy mourning ... When a large group's identity is threatened and power is lost, the healthy group will mourn before reworking their sense of self to accord with a new reality ... there is a cleansing of mind, spirit and psyche to go on after loss ... There is self-examination about our own contribution to the control we are losing, perhaps ending in a rueful recognition that we should never have had that much control. The crisis of mourning well done can morph into a kairos leading to deeper connection with self, others and the Divine.' If Frawley-O'Dea's interpretation is accurate, the institutional refusal to look at what was happening, or to begin to deal with it, had catastrophic consequences for children suffering ongoing sexual abuse.

Frawley-O'Dea says that when mourning is refused we may try to restore manically what has been permanently changed. She writes that the Church was trying to restore old liturgies and clerical dress, with an increase in the saying of the Latin Mass, the return of long trains and birettas and 'a new/old missal in which words are more important than meaning.'

She also claims that sometimes when we deny grief we fix on to something seen as 'other' which we can blame for 'causing' the loss of power. She wonders whether the attempt of the Roman Curia (the Church governing body) to control the American Religious in 2012 was 'a response intended to control their radical work, as they concentrated on service, rather than controlling others. ' Displacing one's own angry feelings on to others and scapegoating are symptoms of avoiding grief on an institutional scale, or letting grief and anger spill out in an unthinking, uncontrolled way which is sometimes directed at some other issue.

Application to CWO

Applying Frawley-O'Dea's message to CWO, it seems that the healthy ways of responding to loss and change are to acknowledge our grief rather than avoid it, not to displace it, unaware, on to others who are not responsible for our predicament (for instance on to other CWO members). Additionally, referring to the Stroebe and Schut Model, the process includes finding a way forward that is not an either/or between emotion or action, but both/and, thus providing a recognition both of the emotions, grief and damage done to us and of constructive ways of responding to the future. The hope is that the combination of both modes will bring:

- a healthy and aware equilibrium that is strong and inclusive

- an emotional integration drawing on the strengths from our experiences, that works to open the doors of a renewed Church to women priests

- an alignment always with Christ's vision for the Church which is responsive to the Spirit and recognises personality and cultural differences

- the attainment of work and prayer for a Church where women's and men's God-given gifts are recognised and shared

- a church where lay people and priests share ministries within their communities, with a priesthood that is characterised by openness and mutual empowerment of everyone's journey to wholeness.

Pope Francis

Pope Francis, still in his early days as Pope, in an interview 'A Big Heart Open to God' given in August 2013, demonstrates a completely different way of thinking from the past. He appears to be acknowledging and facing the problems of the Curia, child abuse and other areas of deep concern, and is encouraging new and old, possibly Vatican II or early church ways of thinking. He says, 'I do not want token consultations, but real consultations' (p.11)... [recognising that] we *should not think that "thinking with the church" means only thinking with the hierarchy of the church.*'(p.12) He goes on to say that 'the thing the church needs most today is the ability to heal wounds and warm the hearts of the faithful.' (p. 14) and 'find new roads' (p.15) and 'the path of collegiality' (p. 18). He says 'the church still lacks a profound theology of women' and (in a sentence which had been left out of the English translation but was quickly re-inserted) 'It is necessary to broaden the opportunities for a stronger presence of women in the church' (p.19). This statement from the Pope is a hopeful sign.

It was soon followed in 2013 by *Evangelii Gaudium*, which includes:

> 104. Demands that the legitimate rights of women be respected, based on the firm conviction that men and women are equal in dignity, present the Church with profound and challenging questions which cannot be lightly evaded. The reservation of the priesthood to males, as a sign of Christ the Spouse who gives himself in the Eucharist, is not a question open to discussion, but it can prove especially divisive if sacramental power is too closely identified with power in general.

However, in September 2013 Pope Francis told reporters that the door was closed to women's ordination. This was initially a blow to CWO but a month later at our Annual Gathering we looked at how we needed to keep trying to open this closed door. At the same time in the weekly Catholic Journal *The Tablet*, the editor Catherine Pepinster wrote, 'A closed door on women's ordination sounds definitive. But is it? Isn't a closed door something you can prise open? Or turn its handle? Indeed, might a man entrusted with the keys of the Kingdom be exactly the one who might be able to open such a door?' (*The Tablet*, 1 February 2014 www.thetablet.co.uk).

CWO's immediate mission is how to recognise the impact of the closed door: how it energises us to help unlock it and prepare for a future through the open door.

The Pope's remarks before, during and after the Extraordinary Synod of the Family, 2014, preparatory to the Ordinary Synod of 2015, give rise to optimism about inclusive ways of regarding the family unit and pastoral directions for supporting those in difficulty. It seems as though Pope Francis is allowing the grief to come out but guiding the Church towards the Restoration Mode. However changes in mind sets as well as structures will be needed to support any renewal.

Conclusion

Olive's short extract is at the beginning of this chapter. Here she writes how she has lived with the wound of not being able to be a priest, yet journeys towards integration:

'Now, nearing sixty, I'm able to trace this wound's progress through my life ... Years have been needed to initiate the process of cleansing the wound thus revealed; to re-orient spiritually, psychologically and theologically; to come to rejoice in how right and just it is to find myself among the Roman Catholic women, now and throughout church history, called to ordained ministry. 'Ministry' has become a key concept for me. What service can I offer to my community with my wound that is, very gradually, being cleansed? Maybe it's to be present and pray in exactly those church settings most hostile to women's call to ordination because there are to be found my brothers and sisters in Christ, both clergy and lay people, who are themselves damaged severely by misguided ecclesiasticism. At the moment I can manage this only on occasion since presence and prayer, to be alongside, in these situations mean a level of vulnerability that I find difficult to bear; though a humorous side to this project has emerged as well. However, I'm increasingly certain that being in a position to let wound speak to wound in prayer does constitute a living out of Christian ministry that can open space for God's gift of resurrection.' (Olive, a member of CWO)

Women and men can develop resilience out of their experience and be able to journey towards a healthy integration of feeling, thought and action which supports them. This may be, for Olive, ministering by her presence and prayer in difficult places and recognising that though she has found some humour to balance her pain she needs to visit difficult places sparingly in order to preserve her equilibrium. Some have found parish and hospital ministry helpful to others and a way of keeping themselves sustained and focused while they await ordained ministry. Some support renewal groups encouraging dialogue like A Call to Action (ACTA), (see ACTA website www.acta.org.uk) or help action groups such as CAFOD and Justice and Peace.

Perhaps one of the greatest supports is to know we are not only a British network but also a worldwide one in WOW, (Women's Ordination Worldwide) which increasingly includes women from developing countries. All our actions and different supports have to be underpinned by the development of a deeper discernment arising from an ongoing personal prayer life, if we wish to become more resilient and integrated. It is for this reason that the next chapter turns to various forms of spirituality in order to help us dive deeper into the mystery of God's ways.

Reflection

Are there times in your life where the Stroebe and Schut Dual Process Model might be helpful to use, on which to reflect:

The ups and downs of life?

Change?

Bereavement

Your experience of being in a renewal or reform group?

Are you able to see whether the Loss or Restoration Mode or the Oscillation/Resilience place is where you are at present? Does that vary?

Might it be helpful to share (only what you want to share) with a trusted friend or fellow person working for renewal?

Can you apply the ways you handled your experience, in the aspect you have chosen, to other challenges in your life?

Can you use this to see how others around you may work with challenging times? Does that help, or not, to understand their reaction better? (Remember we can never know exactly how someone else feels. We can only wonder and explore.)

Bibliography

Fiorenza, E. Schüssler, (1986) *In Memory of Her: A Feminist Theological Reconstruction of Christian Origins.* (Crossroad, New York.)

Frawley-O'Dea, M. *Hierarchy's inability to mourn thwarts healing in church* (May 7 2012 published in National Catholic Reporter. (http://ncronline.org/print/news/accountability/hierarchys-inability-mourn-thwarts-healing-church) downloaded 19/01/2013.

Pepinster, C. writing in *The Tablet* 1 February 2014 (weekly journal published in the UK) see www.thetablet.co.uk

Relf, M., Machin,L. and Archer, N. (2008) *Guidance for Bereavement*

Needs Assessment in Palliative Care (Help the Hospices UK)

Rupp.J, (1999) *Out of the Ordinary* (Ave Maria Press, Indiana)

Stroebe, M., Hansson,R., Stroebe, W., and Schut, H. (Eds. 2001) *Handbook of Bereavement Research* (American Psychological Association)

Other references that may be useful:

Joan Chittister, writer of numerous books, including *Called to Question: A Spiritual Memoir* (2009) (Sheed and Ward). She has a website, Benetvision, and regularly writes for the *National Catholic Reporter* in 'From Where I Stand.'

Mary Grey has written many books about feminist theology and about reform of the Catholic Church. An example is Grey,M., (1997) *Beyond the Dark Night (*Cassell, London.)

Daniel O'Leary is a priest and writer of many books about spirituality. He writes about Celtic and contemplative spirituality. Examples are *Travelling Light: Your Journey to Wholeness* (2001) (Columba Press) and *Begin with the Heart* (2008) (Columba Press). He writes regularly for *The Tablet* and has a website www.djoleary.com

Richard Rohr is a Franciscan priest and writer of numerous books and has a website with daily postings https://cac.org/ His books include *Falling Upward: A Spirituality for the Two Halves of life* (2011) (SPCK), (also 'Loving the Two Halves of Life: The Further Journey in CD, DVD and MP3 forms,) and, *On the Threshold of Transformation Daily Meditations for Men* (2010) (Loyola Press).

Chapter 3

AWAKENING TO SPIRITUAL GROWTH

Seeking spiritual growth is an essential aim for all adults working for a renewed Church, rather being than being an optional extra. It is not usually something that happens naturally in the same way as physical growth. With God's help, we need to awaken and work consciously at spiritual development in our lives, through good and bad times.

This chapter falls into three sections:

- The importance of spiritual growth in working for a renewed Church and campaigning for change.

- Three visions or models of spiritual growth and their application today.

- CWO and personal responses.

Why is spiritual growth important for anyone seeking Church renewal?

Many members of CWO realised from the start the enormous challenge that was facing them and all other renewal groups. Some thought they were working 'only' for structural reform. But the real challenge is that as adult members and believers, each of us has an individual responsibility to grow and deepen our spiritual lives and to work for the renewal of the Church. For CWO this includes women's ordained ministry. Growing with God has been a gradual awakening for some of us. We cannot rely on God, our priests, theologians, or anyone else to do it for us: they can only work with us. This applies to everybody. We not only need to make this realisation our own, but also we have to be aware that without sustaining our spiritual selves and allowing ourselves and others to grow, our campaigning energy will run dry and we will 'burn out'. It is an individual development and at the same time can be nurtured in groups.

Jesus' ministry was one of service to the women and men around him and his followers. His vision was not solely the one we seem to have inherited in the current institutional Church, which has an almost exclusively male, hierarchical, centralised, clerical structure (described in Chapter 4). Jesus ministered to those on the margins: the poor, sinners, widows and other women, lepers and other sick and disabled people, slaves and free, and those outside the Jewish community. He served Jews and Gentiles, women and men, young and old. He constantly clashed with the Jewish religious and legal authorities.

Jesus was continually teaching, praying and forming new communities. These were diverse groups: his closest companions and apostles, who seemed to fluctuate in understanding and loyalty, many deserting Jesus when he was arrested; disciples, who were drawn to his message in varying degrees; and the crowds, who were in turn either following or rejecting him. On Palm Sunday the crowds cheered him but five days later they were choosing Barabbas to live rather than Jesus. As Jesus' ministry developed, many individuals grew spiritually, like his friends Martha, Mary and Lazarus, the Apostles, and Peter their leader, who nevertheless became scared and denied knowing Jesus after his arrest. Some women followers, together with John and a few others who stayed at the Crucifixion, remained loyal despite personal danger. Afterwards, many who had run away returned to Jerusalem and became strengthened and renewed by the Holy Spirit at Pentecost. Out of this tiny group of followers, inspired by God, the Church was formed and developed over the years. We too follow as we each find a way to God. We can waver like many of those early believers.

It seems that the spiritual journey for those wishing to serve is the same mission: listening to God, continuing to learn, accompanying the marginalised, the poor, those suffering discrimination, and the women and men excluded from the church and community; thus we are staying with Jesus when the going gets tough. We waver, are inconsistently both frightened and loyal. Working for renewal demands spiritual strength, as we challenge current Church authorities and structures, in order to stay for the 'long haul'.

Many of us adults still hold only to the religious teachings we learned at school and have not significantly built on those. There is no one way to grow spiritually. We are all different. But every individual spiritual journey includes personal development and trying to understand something of the inner self – in order to be able to connect, as adults, to God and each other. This means that spiritual growth involves an inner individual journey alongside the community journey in our groups and churches. The journey never stops. It includes developing an understanding of our inherited traditions, discerning key beliefs, learning from and transforming personal experience. And, with the inspiration of the Holy Spirit, it means to be able to think for ourselves, to develop an adult conscience, to act with love and justice and encourage each other to grow. Those who speak out believing what they say is just, challenge the status quo and experience the resistance encountered from the powers that be. The authors of this book and our CWO colleagues have met this in different ways as described in these chapters, but we realise how important it is to feed and be sustained by our spiritual lives and to stay connected to God and our communities, in order to keep going.

The terms religious and spiritual

In this chapter, the following broad, and not exclusive, definitions may be helpful. the term 'religious growth' is used to signify the more institutional, public, formal knowledge and intellectual growth about doctrinal teachings, encyclicals (letters), church theological writings and structures. The term 'spiritual' describes the more internal private practices of prayer, meditation, exploration of our hopes, sense of identity and other personal and communal thoughts and practices that may be shared with others.

However, at times it is difficult to distinguish these two aspects, the religious and spiritual, as they are often 'two sides of a coin'. Some spiritual growth is very private, individual and unmediated by other humans. Some is nurtured by group teaching, the experiences of others, and wider influences, such as our personal and cultural background within family, community and society; church structures; the Mass and the sacraments; our own study; and our contemplative prayer lives.

Campaigning groups can be nurturing and supportive but sometimes they can also be as angry, negative and potentially as oppressive as their perceived oppressors. Richard Rohr[8] warns of this danger. He says that 'the process should mirror the vision', which is a reminder to each of us of the way we need to work for renewal. Some people think that we are in danger of putting all our energy into the campaign and not enough into spiritual aspects that might renew ourselves and the Church. This conviction is evident from some of our detractors in the public square and in the media. If 'our process does not mirror our vision', is there a spiritual component that is neglected or missing?

The urgent need for spiritual renewal.
If we discovered soon that we could have women priests and the reforms and renewal we wanted, would we have the spiritual underpinning and maturity to move forward? Or would we be women and men within existing structures, whose liturgies and robes mirrored those associated with priests who have been working in clerical, authoritarian, centralised, hierarchical structures? As we move from a prophetic spirituality derived from exclusion and of the margins, where is the spirituality to underpin a new kind of inclusive

---

[8] Richard Rohr, Franciscan Priest, who runs the Centre for Action and Contemplation, says this consistently in his daily teachings on the internet. See the website https://cac.org/

community ministry sensitive to gender and cultural diversity?

We are potentially faced with a paradox. Many of us say we love the original sacramental vision of the Church and struggle with the centralised, almost exclusively male, hierarchical, clericalised, current Roman Catholic structures. How and where do we find vision, prayer, ideas and language that express the female and male, the non-hierarchical vision of Jesus? And how do we find the more localised 'flatter structure' building blocks for a new community that mirrors more faithfully the Early Church, where women's and men's voices, work and gifts were used, as needed, in smaller, local communities? Ministries were more fluid and women were co-workers alongside men in many communities, (www.wijngaardsinstitute.org; Patrick, 2013, and many others.) Leadership, together with some structure and governance was, and is, required, but there have to be different visions that respect gender and cultural diversity and encourage everyone to use their gifts and get involved. Currently many people feel that they are disengaged, infantilised spectators. Chapter 6 will revisit the concept of future church in greater detail.

What might spiritual growth begin to look like?
Three wise women writers describe ways forward which explore maturing spiritual and connecting themes, and are helpful to us as we awaken to spiritual growth. Ann Patrick (2013) describes an internal spiritual growth movement for women, both religious and lay, and for men, with the intent of moving from an ethic of obedience towards an ethic of responsibility. This requires personal and spiritual growth in order to develop further what she calls 'conscience', which she regards as an ability to discern maturely and responsibly individual and group development. Patrick also describes how Margaret Farley explores a 'framework for love' which relates to a developing religious or secular vocation of justice and compassion that is suffused with love and commitment. Farley does not turn away from criticising gender, race or class hierarchies but suggests compassion and respect must be integral to the way we do this. Una

Kroll, who was a Church of England nun and priest and is now a Catholic and CWO member, has written her autobiography: *Bread not Stones* (2014), which also gives us a helpful way forward. She has found a way of transforming past wounds into a creative present. She uses the phrase 'Unconditional Creative Love' (2014:83-85) to describe how transformation happens, and how she has found she can now work with and understand those opposed to her views as long as there is 'pointing to love'.

These three women individually describe a journey that encourages spiritual growth and maturity in order to develop responsibility, conscience, a calling towards justice and compassion and a way of working with those who may be opposed to us, in a form that helps us to move forward in a congruent, loving way. If we stop listening to and respecting each other, spiritual growth cannot flourish in daily community building where love and justice should work together. We also need to unite in being able to discern together what is possible and distinguish it from what is wrong, unjust, harmful and unworkable. Jesus was able to encourage his disciples to 'brush the dust off their feet' (Mt.10:14; Lk. 9:5) and move on if they judged that dialogue, community building and development were impossible at that moment or in that place. Spiritual growth gives us the developed muscle, conscience or discernment to know how to stay awake to what God is requiring of each of us and to pray and act accordingly. This may mean engaging with, or sometimes walking away from, a situation.

Many of us have learnt from campaigning experience that we are engaged in 'A consciousness revolution ... a spiritual revolution...a wave of transformation,' as well as a structural one, as Ursula King said in 2013.[9] This is a revolution in which there needs to be transformation, both in the perception of women within the Roman

---

[9] Ursula King said this in 2013 at the 'A Call to Action' (ACTA) Conference in Birmingham. ACTA is a UK reform group revisiting Vatican II and calling for dialogue: see www.acalltoaction.org.uk

Catholic Church and in more spiritual terms, a new understanding of authority, governance and leadership. All of these factors have a direct influence on our spiritual growth.

Mary Grey speaks of journeying, dwelling, forming tradition, transforming and dreaming as dimensions of church. She sees the challenge as developing a new approach to fill the divide or tension between the two principal ways of being church: the prophetic and the institutional. In *Beyond the Dark Night* (1997), she names some of these aspects of church. CWO and other renewal groups are often described as predominantly prophetic. Grey is looking at new models of power, authority and leadership, and associates with the prophetic the contemplative and mystical part of spirituality. Grey, like King, is talking of a transformational spiritual way forward for the Church. She writes of the challenge of the institutional church relinquishing its control of the Spirit. 'If the Spirit indeed blows where she will, it would be strange for her not to be found where there is struggle for justice and the flourishing of the well-being of the entire creation' (1997:138). Prophetic action is a charism of the Spirit and what may be required in the northern hemisphere may be different from the south. This is a challenge for a global church.

The need for more Adult Formation or Education

Speaking with many other adults we recognise that a lot of our religious knowledge and spiritual practice was learnt at school and from our families when we were children, and realise that maybe our spiritual lives have not developed much since. Perhaps we learnt our prayers, the catechism, our beliefs, and prepared for the sacraments in our family of childhood, primary school and parish. At secondary school we might have learnt something about Catholic beliefs alongside other religions, some ethical issues about sexual health, euthanasia, world poverty, war etc. If we still go to church, we perhaps receive Communion, hear the sermon and attend occasional talks. Some of us may attend meetings, study days, prayer groups and be aware of religious and social issues that are in the media. Have we built significantly on our childhood foundation?

In my own parish, diocese and in A Call to Action (ACTA) nationally in the UK and locally, there is a growing call from adult Catholics for more accessible adult formation. This means more religious and spiritual education. Many people come to realise that they are still approaching their adult religious life with their childhood knowledge and spirituality, and perhaps are over dependent on their parish priest for their ongoing development. If adult Catholics seek collegiality (in which some of the power and decision making is devolved to bishops and lay people) and try to dialogue with bishops and priests – also one of ACTA's aims - then as responsible adults we need to acquire more religious knowledge underpinned by adult spiritual growth. As Mary R., a CWO member says 'The hungry sheep look up and are not fed. Can we guess how many remain penned in their pews, or how many have voted with their feet, denied any real form of engagement?'[10]

My own consciousness began to be raised when I realised in a sudden 'light bulb' moment in the early 1990s that women might have a calling to be deacons and priests. At that point I had a deep instinctual conviction but I did not have the knowledge, language or adult spiritual development with which to express it or engage in discussion about these ideas, particularly with those opposed to women's ordination. I was a social sciences graduate and a trained social worker, but theology was a different world, or so I thought. I embarked on a Masters' degree of theological study because I had neglected adult formal religious education, and spiritual reading, and lacked the discipline to start without an external framework to guide me. Some adults read independently. They have developed their prayer lives and other spiritual thinking themselves. Some read the

---

[10] This and other statements by CWO members were in response to the question: 'What spiritual ideas and practices keep you in CWO? If your spiritual life has matured, how do you recognise growth?' These comments are interspersed throughout this chapter.

Catholic media like *The Tablet* or *The Pastoral Review* as well as newspapers such as the *Catholic Herald* and *Catholic Times* etc. Or they may have sought courses on feminist and liberation theology, Ignatian, Benedictine or Franciscan spirituality, and other forms of contemplative prayer to help them develop spiritual growth.

The Celtic tradition was mentioned by one CWO group in our internal survey. Celtic spirituality helped them to see 'that it wasn't a male/female issue but seen as creative and in synergy with nature.' Other personal development programmes, such as the Enneagram and Myers-Briggs, have encouraged adults to look at their personality traits and some of the reasons for their emotions and their personal and spiritual behaviour. This might lead some to explore their strengths and 'shadow side' (Jung – see later in this chapter) and different prayer styles. There are many ways of deepening spiritual life. It seems to me it is not appropriate to try and measure spiritual development or dictate how people might approach this as it is an individual journey, albeit often undertaken in community.

Women and men have historically been encouraged to develop differently in the Church, as mentioned in other chapters. The Roman church, after the first centuries, was defined, governed and led by men. Hierarchical systems developed and rational and linear thought was prized. The rational and irrational, male and female, the body and mind, the secular and religious, were seen as either/or entities and a dualism developed from this. which may be defined as a divided either/or way of looking at the world. 'Dualistic thinking will give us... patriarchy instead of community, domination instead of cooperation, and mistrust or fear instead of reconciliation of opposites. It is exactly in our wholeness – not merely one [gender] or the other – that the image of God is revealed and we are healed.'[11]

---

[11] Richard Rohr, 'What Do We Mean by the "Sacred" Character of Gender?' in *Radical Grace,* Winter 2011, Vol. 24, No. 1. It seems to many that wholeness rather than dualism is important for healthy spiritual growth.

Exclusion

The definitive statement of 1994 from Cardinal Ratzinger, who later became Pope Benedict XVI, stating that women's ordination could not be discussed, placed CWO firmly out in the cold in a dualistic (good/bad) structure of who was 'in' and who was 'out'. Many priests and others who had openly supported us and allowed us to use church premises for meetings and liturgies, officially believed they had to stop. Some who spoke out were silenced and suspended, including Bishop Morris in Australia and Father Tony Flannery in Ireland in 2014; the same applied to some CWO members. This kind of exclusion and threat of silencing has had the effect of trying to split CWO from the institutional Church if we persist with our aims. It was not an infallible statement. In dualistic thinking we were not 'good' but 'bad', not 'right' but 'wrong', for disobeying a statement we did not consider valid, a statement that had not been collegially and collectively made. Benedict, when he became Pope, apparently did not reiterate his statement although it still stands.

Pope Francis has spoken of widening women's roles. In the 2013 document *Evangelii Gaudium* (103 & 104) he says that ordination is still closed to women. However, the pastoral style of this document and its wide ranging vision of renewal and the need for other priorities of reform, keep CWO hopeful that the closed door to women's ordination will open when some of the structures and practices within the Church are renewed. What perhaps many people do not realise is how many CWO members live with this exclusion but continue to go to Mass, the sacraments and to pray in churches.

Is spiritual growth a threat to the status quo?

If women and lay men are to develop their spiritual lives this may threaten the existing clerical status quo as it means each person may develop powerfully and unpredictably through tapping directly into a God-given spiritual 'power station' without a clerical intermediary. The wisdom, self-discovery, knowledge and quiet unafraid confidence that spiritual development can bring, may change things! In the Leeds Group we decided to read books, a chapter at a time, and share with each other at monthly meetings as a way of raising our consciousness. Little did we know how threatening this might be! We were reading Paul Collins *Papal Power* (1997), a book which was then under investigation by the Vatican's Congregation for the Doctrine of the Faith. It was a scholarly interesting book about the power of the papacy and how it had become increasingly centralised. While I was reading it in a train in the Midlands, the window was shattered with what was later discovered to be a random airgun pellet. The person reading the next chapter had a similar experience! Knowledge can be dangerous! (The book was later removed from public sale, being considered too subversive.) The book certainly opened the eyes of the Leeds Group about papal history and made us question some of the ideas about the infallibility which Popes sometimes claim when teaching. Although this power is seldom used, many people think that whatever the Pope says is infallible.

Some Visions of Spiritual Growth, and their Application Today

Different models or visions seem to be relevant to different aspects of our spiritual journeying in personal and communal development. It is not the purpose of this chapter to be prescriptive. These thoughts are offered as possibilities for readers to try to deepen their spiritual and personal growth, or help this process if they have already started on this experiential journey. They link in different ways to our awakening to spiritual growth.

1) Belenky,M.F., Clinchy,B.M., Goldberger, N.R., and Tarule,J.M., : *Women's Ways of Knowing: The Development of Self, Voice and Mind.*

In 1997 these four women brought out a new edition of this influential book exploring women's cognitive and psychological development, ten years after its first appearance in print.

These women educators wanted to examine how women develop their ways of knowing by asking women learners and listening carefully to how they developed their thinking about ideas. For the writers the **process** of listening to women was important. They describe five ways of knowing, though these are not to be seen as rigid or prescriptive modes of categorising the responses they received. I have met people who have demonstrated each of these five different developmental ways of knowing, and we may move backwards and forwards through these ways in different situations.

1) Women have no voice.

2) Women listen, use others' knowledge and may see life in polarities.

3) Women develop intuitive ways of knowing and rely on their own thoughts as others have let them down.

4) Women develop a more reasoned knowledge and see people may think differently to themselves.

5) Women begin to integrate knowledge and their integrated voices speak with an authentic voice, combining rational and emotive thought. They can tolerate ambiguity, leave dualism behind, listen to others and have new ideas.

See Appendix 1 for a longer explanation.

It seems to me this model can be used with spiritual as well as educational knowing. Learning and growing are exhibited differently in different people. When women start to ask questions they are moving.

When I read this book I recognised women I had come across in my parish, in meetings, on the Westminster Piazza and outside Leeds (St Anne's) Cathedral in all of the five suggested groupings above. I encountered those with no voice, those expressing only others' views, and giving a gut reaction (often anger) but having no way of explaining why. This happens in groups too.

I believe that within renewal groups we need to try to aim for integrated voices (the 5th group above) where we can have real dialogue with women and men. This is where we can hear each other's voices and arrive at new ideas and visions. We then need the courage and the milieu in which to promote those ideas.

Each of us could read these five groupings and recognise where we might be spiritually on this journey of knowing, both individually and communally. Where we are may change in different contexts. If I am praying I may some days have no voice. Other days I may feel very disconnected from the content of a sermon or a Bishop's Pastoral Letter. Sometimes I may feel empowered to have a real connection to the Mass, a connection that comes from a part of me integrated with God. That integration may also result from a comment from a friend. If someone comes to speak at a meeting, giving current Church teaching about CWO, gay marriage or the Eucharist for the divorced and remarried, I may really have to focus on trying to have 'real talk' rather than be told what I should be thinking and doing, or reacting by retreating or getting angry. I may react instinctively to the speaker's wish instead of trying to combine rational and emotive thought. The fifth grouping of 'integrating the voices' would be about trying to listen to each other, exploring ideas constructively and perhaps together developing new ways forward.

The model of Belenky and her colleagues is useful for all women and men to consider, because of both its methodology in the collaborative group processes it uses and for the phases of knowing it describes. It is useful to discover the 'disconnect' that goes on sometimes in discussion and action in Church circles. This model traces a journey from silence to integrating different, developing voices. It seems to me that this model illustrates a way of accompanying each other towards integration. The potential for integration is in each of us and those we serve. It helps us to integrate with each other. Jesus came to be with each of us in community.

2) *The Interior Castle* of St Teresa of Avila.

This vision or model is from 1577. Teresa has been called a psychological mystic because the journey to God, for her, is also a journey to self-knowledge and development (Welch, 1982:2). She was a great reforming saint who in 1990 was recognised as a Doctor of the Church. She has given us one of the earliest visions of spiritual growth written down by a woman. It was developed as an individual journey by a nun within a Carmelite community. Although she travelled around to other Carmelite convents her Order was enclosed. Her 'crystal castle' is a circular symbol of the self. The spiritual journey moves from the outer courtyard to the centre of the castle. Her journey has seven dwelling places. It traces increasing spiritual and psychological development, (through self-knowledge), to growing union with God. We progress from knowledge to ' a lived and living experience' (John Venard, 1974). There are many subdivisions in each stage, something which recognises the uniqueness of the individual journey towards the light, to God. It seems to me that is should <u>not</u> be seen as a stratified linear model but rather a circular dynamic journey, filled with symbolic images – water, the butterfly, devils and serpents – to represent encounters on this circular journey.

The first three dwelling places or mansions are preparatory stages of prayer, a relationship with God, perseverance and self-discipline. The fourth is a transition from active to contemplative prayer.[12] In the

---

[12] She uses at this point a helpful image of two troughs of water to illustrate the difference between active meditation and mystical prayer. She writes, 'These two troughs are filled with water in different ways; with one the water comes from far away through many aqueducts and the use of much ingenuity; with the other [trough,] the source of the water is right there, and the trough fills without any noise. If the spring is abundant, as is this one we are speaking about, the water overflows once the trough is filled, forming a large stream. There is no need of any skill … but water is always flowing from the spring' (IV chapter 2.2). John Welch (1982: 64) describes the difference. With the first trough prayer begins with the person and ends with God. With the second trough prayer begins with God

fifth dwelling place there is a deepening contemplative prayer of union and Teresa uses the image of the silkworm dying in order to become a butterfly: dying and rising in union with Christ. In dwelling place six there is an intensification of union which she describes as a 'spiritual marriage.' The preparation for this involves trial, pain and joy. In the seventh dwelling place the union is completed in the Trinity. There is now peace. And then Teresa describes being propelled back into the world: 'This is the reason for prayer, my daughters, the purpose of this spiritual marriage: the birth always of good works, good works' (VII chapter 4.6). She describes spiritual marriage – union - 'it is like what we have when a little stream enters the sea: there is no means of separating the two.' (VII chapter 2.4).

Carl Jung, Psychiatrist and Psychoanalyst.

Though some of St Teresa's ideas and words come from her enclosed 16th century community, 20th century Carl Jung also uses some similar imagery. Welch (1982) looks at Teresa's internal journey and imagery alongside the psychoanalytical and symbolic work of Jung. Jung uses water as a symbol for the unconscious, while the butterfly image of death and resurrection serves as an allegory of the psyche emerging through a series of transformations. Welch sees commonalities in their work: Jung sees journeying as human development, while Teresa describes the journey through the *Interior Castle* as spiritual and personal development, overcoming obstacles on the journey.

A feature of Jung's work is the concept of our 'shadow side', the parts of our personality we do not like or may try to deny. Part of Jungian psychology is to become conscious of our shadow side so we can recognise our shadows / personality difficulties and address them, accept some of them and work through others to further development. If we do not do this, shadows can rule our lives. The

---

and ends with the person. This fourth dwelling is the beginning of true mystical prayer and the water that is then a large stream is an ocean by the time the sixth mansion is entered.

notion of the shadow side of self can perhaps be seen in the 'devils' in Teresa's castle. She encourages her Sisters to look at their own faults rather than concentrating on those of others. Developing insight and working on one's own shadow side is an important part of spiritual development.

Welch describes the castle as an image of wholeness – a circular castle. Jung noticed that a sphere was a symbol of wholeness and at one stage daily drew a mandala (the Sanskrit word for circle) to represent his state of self on that day. He used these circles to work on his own development.

It seems to me that anyone in a renewal group is on a journey of self-discovery alongside the spiritual journey, and that acknowledging our shadow side is key. How we respond to resistance and disagreement is important. If we play out our own internal conflict and stumbling points and are unaware of how this impact on ourselves and others, we will repeat them and become alienated and exhausted. This is explored further in Richard Rohr's work below.

The relevance of St Teresa of Avila's work today

Teresa's journey can be travelled by all of us, women and men: 'In sum, my Sisters, what I conclude with is that we shouldn't build castles in the air. The Lord doesn't look so much at the greatness of our works as at the love with which they are done' (VII chapter 4.15). The journey she envisages is not only for the individual: 'The view from the centre of Teresa's castle is much more world-embracing than the ego-constructed view from the periphery. The journey through the castle will result in more, not less, social interest and activity.' (Welch 1982:188.)

If adult spirituality is about journeying to the centre of ourselves and the community we serve, Teresa's model is significant. Welch's commentary on *The Interior Castle* concludes with a thought relevant for women and men in the Church today. He describes Teresa's spiritual marriage as an image symbolising our longing for union with the 'other.' This term embraces the 'other' within ourselves, the 'other' human being, and the 'other' as God. In terms of the person, otherness is often seen in the relationship between women and men, the feminine and masculine. Real dialogue between the two, Welch believes, brings about transformation. (Personally I also believe this applies to unions between women and between men.)

3) *The Two Halves of Life,* from Richard Rohr [13] the American Franciscan of the Centre of Action and Contemplation (https://cac.org/)

Rohr writes about the Two Halves of life in spiritual terms. First Half of Life spirituality is about establishing ourselves as adults, belonging to our church and community, raising children, working, and having a way of thinking that is about developing our identity, knowing the rules and finding out how life works. Our religious faith in the First Half of Life might be more about observing laws and perhaps emphasising membership of the institutional Church. Our perception of that Church, and its view of itself, may become exclusive, only including those who follow the rules. Rohr says that is why Jesus walks to those marginalised and at the edges of society. He goes towards the excluded people.

Rohr describes the Second Half of Life as a spiritual growth that develops from dissatisfaction about First Half of Life. We recognise that there is 'a wound at the heart of things.' So in the Second Half of Life our sadness and struggles (and, I would include, a calling to women's ordination) make us take a different spiritual journey. Rohr claims that most of us have to have this different journey forced on us, because spiritual growth is challenging: 'The rug has to be pulled out from beneath our game, so we redefine what balance really is.' He

---

[13] Rohr, *On the Threshold of Transformation: Daily Meditations for Men* (2010: 267) and *Falling Upward: A Spirituality for the Two Halves of Life* (2011), *Loving the Two Halves of Life: The Further Journey* CD, DVD and MP3. See his website https://cac.org/ and bibliography.

says however that we need to know the rules of the First Half in order to be able to break them in the Second Half, if this is what we each discern to be the right thing to do. We realise in the Second Half of Life that we need to lose our dualistic thinking. We become more inclusive, 'self –emptying' and understanding of others.

Rohr's Second Half of Life bears comparison with St Teresa's move towards union, and Belenky and colleagues' fifth way of Integrated Voices. The 'Other' becomes understood and included or integrated in to our lives.

Rohr says that the Ten Commandments could be seen as suited to First Half of Life and the Beatitudes more fitted to inclusive Second Half of Life Spirituality, a statement that deserves reflection.

Rohr's vision allows people to work on spiritual development from 'the place where they are at.' It contrasts with some of Rohr's other work on growth, which is more structured and linear (compare it with his *Stages of Growth*' lecture given in York, UK in 2007.) Linear and structured models might be described as more 'male' theological thinking. However, he has some spirituality courses devised especially for men to help them to release their feelings, experience emotions and begin to 'think outside of the box' (mentioned earlier by Myra Poole). Rohr has identified that male and female spirituality may initially be different but that Second Half of Life spirituality is for both women and men to develop.

A communal spirituality for renewal groups?

It appears to me that the Rohr model (First Half, Second Half of Life), although individual, can also be experienced as a communal spirituality for CWO and others in renewal groups. Whatever our chronological age, adult spirituality perhaps requires us to travel into Second Half of Life spirituality. Does our mission send us beyond the safe places? Do we have to challenge dualistic thinking? Do we grasp the 'woundedness' at the heart of ourselves and the institutional Church? (See chapter 2.) Do we have to empty ourselves to grow?

Here then is a spiritual challenge for each of us: how do we know our 'wound', and how do we live with it and use it to transform ourselves and our work? I think most of us are not being asked to sit with our wound and do nothing and let it be; but how we use it in a spiritually mature way is for each of us to discern and 'know' (Belenky et al.). How can it transform us and our calling? How do we avoid dualistic thinking in our discussion – the notion that my view is right, your thought is wrong, less radical, less compassionate or whatever? Many of us do feel a calling to stick with the struggle for the long haul and move it forward. Once injustice and discrimination have been noticed, they can't be ignored – just as you can't be just a little bit pregnant ...

It seems this First and Second Half of Life model echoes with the Stroebe and Schut process explored in Chapter 2. Loss or change forces a new equilibrium that is growth. Moving through Rohr's Second Half of Life requires this too. He speaks of the 'necessary suffering' that we each have. For CWO this might be church authorities disregarding our vocation or our work for renewal, relationship failure, sadness, illness and other difficulties. He says that suffering has the potential either to edge us forward, or to make us dig in and either 'fall upward' or 'keep falling' (*Falling Upward: A Spirituality for the Two Halves of Life* 2012). The Second Half of Life is a place outside our comfort zone, a place of journey where we listen to God. We may go beyond rules and safe places but we need to know those rules before we decide whether they are unjust.

New compassionate, loving, inclusive ways of thinking and action ideally take the place of unjust rules and paralysis caused by the institutional rejection of women's gifts. Rohr says 'This "wound at the heart of life" shows itself in many ways in different lives, but your holding and "suffering" of it ... makes you patient, loving, hopeful and compassionate.' This is an aim is to be hoped for. This, and the dying to self, and onward development, illustrated in Teresa's model, align with the kind of prophetic spirituality that CWO members try to journey towards, aiming for women's ordained ministry in a renewed Church. This includes others seeking personal and institutional renewal. Praying and campaigning patiently and compassionately is hard. I think that impatience for action and justice is sometimes needed lest we develop a 'doormat' mentality, while others may take advantage of our willingness to wait. The discernment that comes from our spiritual development will help us to decide the right path and action.

Rohr has said that in the First Half of Life, in psychological terms, we have to develop an ego. Jung also recognises that we need to develop a healthy ego to achieve identity and adult autonomy. The earlier stages of 'ways of knowing' (Belenky et al) require psychological growth in order to develop individual thoughts and the validity of thinking for oneself (and then others). St Teresa's journey towards union also predicates an idea of personal development that can sustain difficulties.

However, St. Teresa and Rohr both require a 'dying to self' in order to move towards union with God. It seems that Belenky et al also require it to a limited extent, in the sense that in order to have integrated talk we need self-awareness and be able to listen to others' ideas. This may require us in 'real talk' to integrate others' ideas into our own, or even substitute them for our own. But key values and ideas are non-negotiable.

These models suggest a way of letting go so that we are ready to serve each other. Some ideas about a church framework that will help us serve and support each other are described in Chapter 6.

CWO and Personal Responses

CWO is a group of prayer, spiritual renewal and campaign. Many of us have completed theology courses, developed liturgy and have pastoral experience (where permitted). We also have relevant experience in social work, counselling, teaching, administration, management, nursing, finance and charity work. This work experience is underutilised in the current Church. Some lay men would also agree that their work experience is underused.

I am spiritually sustained by being able to go to Mass. This reconnects me to God and my parish community. The Eucharist is the essence of my belief, and it helps to restore me and work for an equilibrium that is centring for my day. I recognise it is partly because I am in a lay-involved parish with a collaborative priest that I am able to gain sustenance from within the Roman Catholic Church.

However I cannot be over-dependent on my Parish Priest to be sustained. Being closely connected to a parish community is not possible for some in CWO and for other disaffected Catholics. Like everyone else I know I cannot consistently sustain the levels of spiritual maturity that Rohr writes about. I have not reached the Seventh Dwelling Place or constantly 'integrate the voices.' I am sometimes going round in circles and finding that the same snares trap me! My ways of knowing (Belenky and colleagues) vary, but I think I listen better to other people's modes of expressing their ways of knowing and sometimes mine is integrated. Some days I operate out of an immature, insecure place, but I think that knowing what spiritual growth and maturity might mean facilitates its recognition even though this is transient. Getting glimpses of others' journeys and connecting with them helps me on my own spiritual journey. It feeds me and helps me to be more compassionate and understanding with others who have challenges.

An example of 'Integrated Voices'

I would like to give a personal example of 'Integrating the Voices.' A number of us in CWO have given interviews to TV and radio, and have written letters and articles. I have done a number of interviews where I have recognised that the time slot is very brief and I have needed to talk in headlines, giving references to Church teachings and events and also to be prepared to be challenged by the interviewer. Hence it becomes a didactic conversation (or Procedural Thought as Belenky et al might describe it). Pat Brown, another CWO member, has also experienced this.

However we both remember one joint interview where we thought we had given our diverse but complementary thoughts as part of a discussion, and we considered the essence and process of CWO had come through as well as our reasoned ideas and 'integrated voices.' We were having a conversation with Becky Milligan for BBC Radio 4 and she skilfully edited an hour's conversation to about eight minutes, which accurately reflected the longer interview. Pat and I believed we were able to talk about CWO and bring out the different points that we wanted to make in a non-threatening and friendly way, with the spiritual ideas behind them. The two sets of ideas wove together. I spoke more about the history and theology of CWO and Pat emphasised feminism and issues of justice. We sounded reasonable and natural but committed, and we thought that this was more persuasive and 'real talk' for listeners than some of the other interviews we have done. Some of it was repeated on Christmas Day to provide a different point of view from someone else's perspective, so it was then being used in a more Procedural way. Because we had been interviewed in this way and we felt confident to say what we believed, we thought it more effective and thought provoking for the listener.

Inclusive language

Many of us in the pews have been concerned that we are now compelled to use the New Translation of the Mass (International Commission on English in the Liturgy (ICEL) 2011, known as the New Liturgy of the Mass (see Chapter 5). This liturgy is closely translated from the Latin and retains exclusive language, which means here that exclusively male nouns and pronouns are used and God the Father, Son and Spirit and humans are all represented as male. This completely excludes the female element of creation and as a female I am referred to as 'man' and 'he.' It uses set prayers and prescribes set forms of behaviour for parts of the Mass.

Once exclusive language has been noticed, it cannot be ignored. Some members of CWO, (P.A.R.A. and P. from the CWO survey) and those in other CWO groups speak of the inclusive liturgies CWO uses as a source of sustenance, growth and inclusion. By inclusive liturgy I mean not only one where the language is inclusive but also one which does not model a 'them and us' picture of priests saying Mass as distant figures on the inside while lay people are at the edge. An inclusive liturgy does not imply that the priest alone is doing the important action and we somehow are spectators from an inferior lay and women's place.

CWO Liturgy

CWO groups use biblical readings, together with a host of varied other material, including books such as *Making Liturgy: Creating Rituals for Worship and Life* (2001) (See bibliography for some examples). Different forms of meditation, days of reflection and our annual CWO Retreat are spiritually helpful. The CWO Retreat, held in tranquil surroundings, is self-directed: we minister to each other, with spiritual contributions from the participants. There is also the opportunity to relax and have some fun!

The London and Leeds groups in particular have built up many liturgical resources (some of these are mentioned in the Bibliography). Many groups have used liturgies drawn from work by CWO members and authors such as Joyce Rupp, Nicola Slee, Janet Morley, and the poetry of Mary Oliver. The quarterly publication *Network* of our sister group Women Word, and Spirit and many others have provided inspiration. These sources sit alongside scriptural readings and thoughts and prayers of some of the saints, including St Therese of Lisieux who wrote in her diaries of her wish to be a priest (*Story of a Soul* 8 September, 1896), while Saints Teresa of Avila and Catherine of Siena talk about ministry in a way that relates to priesthood. Readings from the women mystics, especially Julian of Norwich, are sometimes included. The Wild Goose Resources from the Iona Community and other ecumenical sources are sometimes used.

Some groups have created songs, visual resources, and litanies. As people have grown in confidence they have developed their own liturgies, writing their own material and encouraging each other to contribute ad lib. They find the confidence to explore the Bible and include readings apt for a particular occasion or they may use the regular Readings of the Day as well as non-scriptural readings. For many years the Leeds Group have held a regular Eucharistic Liturgy when they meet. Each member decides individually about what the event means to them: whether they are participating in a memorial of the Last Supper, a fellowship gathering or a Eucharist. Those present often anoint each other's hands and heads, as a symbol of healing, strength and affirmation.

The careful creative spiritual process of making liturgy (Eucharistic or otherwise) is key to inclusive, diverse group worship. For people who have had no voice in this sphere before, it is empowering to honour experience, and once people find a voice, there can be an outpouring of prayerful creativity. Choices of set or specially created texts are important. (Examples are given in Appendix 2.) Music, dance, symbols, pictures and flowers are important for many participants. They are especially significant on occasions when not everyone can speak the same language; they also afford an opportunity to recognise and honour cultural practices and diversity of experience. There are endless possibilities for liturgy: liturgical seasons, cycles of the year, Mary, the Saints (both those officially canonised and known good people who have died). There may be family celebrations, acknowledgement of tough intractable times for those who are bereaved, anxious, unemployed, mentally ill, asylum seekers, survivors of abuse, world disasters ... The list is endless. Informal, impromptu liturgy may be helpful for both the churched and the unchurched when it is responsive to immediate local and international need.

Quite frequently we hear of a service being held in the context of a community where there has a local need, such as severe flooding, a death in a road traffic accident, a disappearance or even a murder. The creation of a liturgy is increasingly seen as comforting or cathartic, and a way for the community to come together in their distress and grief with a structure that may include prayers, music, photographs and reminiscence from those who wish to speak; sometimes there is celebration of the gift of particular person. Participants and ministers have said that this kind of liturgy also helps to defuse feelings of anger and powerlessness and can start a process of learning to live with what has happened. Roadside shrines marking a local traffic accident have been helpful to some people. Other occasions include thanksgiving with family and friends for the survival of a baby who nearly died, a 100th birthday in a care home, renewing the commitment of vows: all life events such as these bring an opportunity to express emotion, find strength, reflect and connect to faith and each other.

If different religious denominations and faiths come together and do not feel they can share a Eucharist or other common ritual, then a liturgy that celebrates common humanity and can be shared is significant. Options are endless. I know of one organisation, at least, that follows a reconciliation service with a surprise party. The juxtaposition of these two different modes of involvement may be recalled many years later, with powerful effect. Pain and reconciliation followed by something more celebratory can sometimes be healing, though care needs to be taken as sometimes the distress is too immediate and overwhelming, so that any fun element needs to be deferred until a later occasion. Discernment is necessary.[14]

---

[14] An example of creating a specific liturgy for particular circumstances is illustrated in *Not for Sale: Raising Awareness, Ending Exploitation: Churches Alert to Sex Trafficking Across Europe* (Pemberton, Myers and Berry, 2007). This contains prayers, some adapted, some not, and scripture readings for people who have been subject to human trafficking and sexual abuse. There are many powerful readings, testimonies, reflections, hymns

Some of this description of personal liturgy may seem simple and obvious. However I can give a personal example which emphasised for me how many have been disempowered from believing they could create liturgy. I remember clearly how in her seventies, my mother (a wife, grandmother, ballet dancer, writer, retired NHS Practice Manager, and actor, so no stranger to public performance) being overjoyed at creating the (Bidding) 'Prayers of the People' for the first time in her life at a Eucharistic Liturgy with Sue, a member of CWO. Somehow, despite my mother's considerable gifts, she had not been encouraged to use her creativity at the Masses which she attended every week of her life. There was a 'disconnect' between private prayer, and domestic and public church based-liturgy. My step-father, who had previously been a priest, had felt he needed to accept that'Father' planned the prayers and read all the responses. My mother had frequently read at Mass, in her beautiful trained voice, the prayers devised by the priest, but somehow had never thought that her faith, life experience and great ability to empathise with others' experience, had equipped her to write and give voice to her own prayers publicly. Such an involvement was not allowed in that parish – ironically, considering given that these prayers are termed the 'Prayers of the People (or Faithful).'

Over the years CWO have learned how to devise and carry out liturgy by doing it. We have all developed confidence in believing we have the God-given right, as God's People, to find or compose readings, songs, poetry and prayers. The ritual strengthens us. It empowers us to keep going. It gives us experience and confidence in preparation for a time in the future when we may be leading liturgy in a ministry

---

and poetry. It includes a prayer of 'Male Repentance' which is in the form of a litany. Each verse starts 'We (men) repent ...' (Sven-Gunnor Liden, p.79.) It is a book to use in connection with the healing process which is a crucial part of most liturgy. This book also seems a helpful response to raising awareness of peoples' situations in a traumatic area of life that many people in wider society have only recently become more aware of.

role, or currently, for me, as a hospital chaplaincy volunteer.

Some CWO responses about spiritual growth

When CWO members were asked about recognising their own spiritual growth, some have responded in a way which shows that they found this growth had surprised them and was only recognised retrospectively. One said, 'I suspect all of us remain something of a curate's egg with some parts further along than others.' Some saw it 'as growing from a child-like acceptance to thinking for oneself with God working through us rather than outside of us.' Some said they could recognise growth in other members. One mentioned that prayer had become more meaningful for her and that she felt the presence of the Holy Spirit giving her courage to speak out, a feeling shared by others.

Along the way one group said 'Jesus challenged the status quo and we challenge the status quo in his name.' Olive, a CWO member, has said that we recognise that we are different in the way we view the future of the Church and the role of ordained ministry, but we share common ground in the spiritually vital need for full participation by women. What she says suggests that our spiritual practices bring us together. (This seems particularly important for a campaigning group where a dynamic of struggle and exclusion can divide.)

When asked what spiritual ideas might help others, one person said: 'Pray as you can and not as you can't.' Another volunteered: 'All you can do is drop the pebble and hope the ripples reach the bank.' Others find the Mass and Eucharist a healing community experience. One said: 'The Eucharist: this provides a balance for the day. This transcends the wound of being excluded from participating in saying the Mass myself or having a more formal pastoral role in a team ministry in such a community. I know that will come.' A CWO group said 'Sowing the seeds but not necessarily seeing the fruit.' This was also said by Ianthe, one of our CWO founders, in a CWO website video clip (www.catholic-womens-ordination.org.uk). There is a deep spiritual solidarity, a combination of pain with hope, expressed by many CWO members who share this idea. Several people wanted to develop pastoral gifts such as 'listening well', so that when opportunities arise we can be responsive and self-giving.

The prophetic and the institutional: some concluding comments

It is to be hoped that Pope Francis' mission to help the poor and to counter inequality will bring a realisation that these groups include women. Unjust structures and unequal access for women remain at every level within the institutional Church. The Pope's radical approach to poverty, his pastoral, responsive and people-centred attitude, are promising, as indicated by the fact that he is encountering resistance in certain areas of the Church. However, real substantial acknowledgement of women's role in the Church needs to be addressed soon, and the closed door opened.

We take our guide from the life of Jesus on the margins: 'to give good news to the destitute...to set the oppressed free' (Lk. 4:18.) We offer our experience. We search in the Bible for the sparse mentions of the life of Mary and the other women in the Gospels. We are called from within our communities. The vision we have for ordained women's ministry is to be with people in the margins and to serve those around us, something as counter-cultural in Jesus' time as it is in the 21st century.

Reflection

Think about a person or event you would like to recall in a liturgy. In devising a liturgy think of key events, aspects of their personality or actions that might give you ideas to create a liturgy.

Where will it be? Who will gather with you?

Will you have readings, music, pictures, a power point presentation, flowers? What symbols might you use?

Who might lead or take part in different sections of the Liturgy?

BIBLIOGRAPHY

Belenky, M.F., Clinchy, B.M., Goldberger, N.R., Tarule, J.M., (Eds.) (1986/1997) *Women's Ways of Knowing: The Development of Self, Voice and Mind* (Basic Books, New York.)

Pope Francis (2013) *Evangelii Gaudium: Apostolic Exhortation of Pope Francis.* www.vatican.va

Grey, M. (1997) *Beyond the Dark Night: A Way Forward for the Church* (Cassell, London and Virginia.)

King, N. (2004) *The New Testament* (Kevin Mayhew, Suffolk)

Kroll, U. (2014) *Bread not Stones: The Autobiography of an Eventful Life* (Christian Alternative Books / John Hunt Publishing)

Mc Ewan, D., Pinsent,P., Pratt, I., and Seddon, V. (2001) (Eds.) *Creating Rituals for Worship and Life*) (The Pilgrim Press Ohio and Canterbury Press Norwich.)

Patrick, Anne E. (2013) *Conscience and Calling: Ethical Reflections on Catholic Women's Vocations (*Bloomsbury, London and New York.)

Pemberton, Myers and Berry (2007) *Not for Sale: Raising Awareness, Ending Exploitation: Churches Alert to Sex Trafficking Across Europe.* (Inspire, Peterborough.)

Rohr,R. (2011) *Falling Upward: A Spirituality for the Two Halves of Life* (SPCK)

Rohr, R. *Loving the Two Halves of Life: the Further Journey* CD, DVD and MP3 and on https://cac.org/

Rohr, R. (2010) *On the Threshold of Transformation: Daily Meditations for Men* (Loyola Press)

Rohr, R. (2007) 'Stages of Growth' Lecture given at the University of York St John, in York UK

Rohr, R. (2011) 'What do we Mean by the 'Sacred' Character of Gender?' *Radical Grace, Winter 2011 Vol.24 No.1*

Rupp, J. (2000) *Out of the Ordinary* (Ave Maria Press, Indiana)

Venard, J. Aka John - Venard Smith (1974) *The Interior Castle: St Teresa of Avila* (Koinonia, Manchester.)

Welch, J. (1982) *Spiritual Pilgrims: Carl Jung and Teresa of Avila* (Paulist Press, New York.)

Other Helpful Books

Gateley, E. (1998) *A Mystical Heart* (Crossroad)

Gateley, E. (2000) *Growing into God* (Sheed and Ward.)

Grey, M. (2000) *The Outrageous Pursuit of Hope: Prophetic Dreams for the 21st Century* (Darton, Longman and Todd, London)

Harris, M. (1989) *The Seven Steps of Women's Spirituality* (Bantam Books New York)

Morley, J. (1994) *All Desires Known* (Morehouse)

Oliver, M. (2007) *Thirst* (Beacon USA and Bloodaxe Northumberland.)

Oliver, M. (2004) *Wild Geese: Selected Poems* (Beacon USA and Bloodaxe Northumberland)

Poole, M. (2001) *Prayer, Protest, Power. The Spirituality of Julie Billiart Today* (Canterbury Press Norwich.)

Ruether,R.R. (1994) *Gaia and God: An Ecofeminist Theology of Earth Healing* (Harper-Collins)

Ruether, Rosemary Radford. (1993) *Sexism and God Talk* (Beacon Press)

Slee, N. (2004) *Praying Like a Woman* (SPCK)

Slee, N. (2011) *Seeking the Risen Christa* (SPCK London)

Appendix 1

Belenky, M.F., Clinchy B.M., Goldberger, N.R., and Tarule, J.M., (Eds.) (1986/1997)

Women's Ways of Knowing: The Development of Self, Voice and Mind (Basic Books New York.)

A fuller description of the Five Ways of Knowing:

The first way of knowing: They found some women had no voice. Women were silent and let others speak for them.

The second way of knowing: Women listened as a way of knowing. Theirs was Received Knowledge, not creating knowledge of their own. They learnt from an external authority outside of themselves and life was often seen in terms of polarities e.g. good or bad, which was dualistic thinking.

The third group of women showed Subjective Knowledge. These people had developed an intuitive way of knowing: a gut reaction. They might be thinking for themselves but Belenky et al would claim they have not yet developed a coherent, reflective moral authority which they would use to weigh things up. Some of these women had started to rely exclusively on their own thoughts and feelings because they had been let down by others.

The fourth group had developed Procedural Knowledge (The Voice of Reason). They were giving a more reasoned reflection in their work than perhaps earlier in their development. They were developing an ability to give a conscious and systematic analysis of an idea. They were seeing people might have a right to different opinions.

The fifth and final way of knowing is Constructed Knowledge: Integrating the Voices

To learn to speak in a unique and authentic voice, women must 'jump outside 'the frames and systems of authorities, provide and create their own frame' (p.134) The writers noticed women were attempting to integrate knowledge that they felt was intuitively important, with knowledge learned from others. They were combining rational and emotive thought. They could tolerate ambiguity and leave dualistic thinking 'and move beyond systems, putting systems to their own service.' Women can hear their own voices as well as others and arrive at new ideas.

Appendix 2

Further Liturgy

There are many helpful ways of connecting to God and each other in liturgy. Rosemary Radford Ruether's *Sexism and God Talk* (1983) gave me my first glimpse of what good, theologically informed, inclusive, personalised, imaginative new liturgy could be. Inclusive liturgy once heard can never be discounted in liturgy, including pastoral sensitivity. Liturgies can be personal and relevant to a particular group. An example may illustrate this in liturgy for an older woman from *Creating Rituals for Worship and Life* (Eds McEwan, Pinsent, Pratt and Seddon 2001.) 'Croning: Celebrating a Seventieth Birthday '(166-169). The process in this liturgy is honouring the transition to later life and the wisdom of the older woman.

The Liturgy includes:

A candle lit for each decade

A specially written song

A version of Ecclesiastes Chapter 3 adapted for the life of the person: 'There is a season...A time to be born...'

Discussion takes place in pairs about what has happened in the last decade, and a hope of personal change for each person taking part, in the future.

An honouring of the older person being 'croned.'

A lighting of an eighth candle for the next decade and a final prayer and dance.

Making Liturgy (pp166-9).

Joyce Rupp in *A Ritual for Ageing*, 2000 (p.47) also has *'A Liturgy for Older Women'*. Hers, on this occasion is an individual reflection. It includes Psalm 71: 'God, from my youth you have taught me...' It also involves reflecting on photos from each decade and creating a psalm from one's own life experience of ageing.

These are two examples of group and individual creation of liturgy for older women. They both happen to be for women by women. There may be occasions when liturgy for men by men is appropriate, or liturgy prepared by and for a mixed group.

Chapter 4
AWAKENING: TO THE 'DEFECTIVE' TRADITION ON WOMEN

'I would rather ordain a cat than a woman'
(words said to Myra on the Westminster Piazza)

'The Catholic Church remains the chief stronghold of sexual inequality, domination and exclusiveness,' Alice Abadan, (an influential speaker in St Joan's International Alliance, 1911, the first woman's Church reform group in Britain). (See below).

The first of these statements stunned some people when Myra quoted it on the radio. Many reacted violently against it, saying or thinking that it could not be true and must be exaggerated. Unfortunately, this is not the case. But from where, deep down in the psyche, does such a phrase emerge? History tells us why, but in order to be understood, any writing, past or present, has to be put into context, coupled with the knowledge of who wrote it and out of what experience. This kind of statement, based on erroneous interpretations of scripture and history, has echoes throughout the ages until the present day. Attitudes like this have caused tremendous suffering to so many women, as testified by Aruna Gnanadason in her book *No Longer Secret: The Church and Violence Against Women* [15]

Although there are many accounts of the historical background which are much fuller than is possible here, it is important to remind ourselves of the myths propagated against women that have

---

[15] WCC Publications, (1993), published during the Church of England's decade on women (1988-1998).

endured so long in all Christian denominations. From Eve onwards, women have been burdened with being the cause of original sin, and depicted too often in scripture and theology in a polarised way, as either a harlot or a virgin.

The Church, in its official teaching office, has long taught that women are inferior to men, at least in this life, though not in the eschatological perspective of the next life. 'Defective' is a word associated with women, while homosexuals are considered 'disordered'. So if a woman is 'gay' she is both 'defective' and 'disordered' according to this teaching – a double whammy!

The Cuckoo's egg tradition and women's ordination-an explanation

John Wijngaards, a tireless scholar, has founded an online website www.wijngaardsinstitute.org that originates from his concern as to why the Church has been so resistant to the idea of women deacons and priests[16]. His book, *The Ordination of Women in the Catholic Church: Unmasking a Cuckoo's Egg Tradition* (Canterbury Press, 2001) takes a novel approach to this question. In it he explains that there grew up in the Christian tradition two different interpretations on gender differences: the Graeco-Roman androcentric position of Aristotle, where the male is believed to be the summit of human creation; and the scriptural baptismal tradition as displayed in Galatians 3:27-2, where Paul claims: 'For as many of you as were

---

[16] This website has grown immensely and is now translated into many languages. It is the best website in existence both on the subject of women and priesthood and on other topics related to renewal in the Church, such as the question of authority in the Church. Wijngaards has literally devoted the last half of his life to this research, thus performing a great service to all women and men in the Church. His work reflects his knowledge and interest in developing countries. He was a missionary in India for a considerable time. This website is an invaluable resource both now and for future generations. Any information not provided in this book can be found on it.

baptised into Christ have put on Christ. There is neither Jew nor Greek, there is neither slave nor free, there is neither male nor female; for you are all one in Jesus Christ'.

Unfortunately the Graeco-Roman tradition seems to have taken precedence over the real Christian tradition, while the *Epistle to Timothy* (which may not be Paul's as such) continues this underlying bias against women, a bias that has endured to the present day: 'I permit no woman to teach or to have authority over a man; she is to keep silent...she will be saved by child rearing' *(1 Tim 2)*.

Wijngaards explains his theory as follows:

> Cuckoos not only lay their eggs surreptitiously in the nests of other birds; they cunningly lay imitation eggs of the hosts. In Britain for instance, cuckoos can variously lay eggs that resemble in spots and colours the eggs of dunnocks, redstarts, sparrows and warblers. The host bird remains unaware of the fact that the foreign egg has been added ... The cuckoo chick has developed a fiendish form of behaviour known as 'nest mate ' eviction ... Within a few hours of hatching, the blind, naked, young cuckoo displays a strong urge to evict any objects ... it heaves the object over the rim of the nest ... Within 24 hours of hatching, the young cuckoo has the nest and the attention of the foster parent to itself ... For many years women had served in a number of ministries, including the sacramental diaconate. It all went overboard. The priestly vocations of women were suppressed. ... a cuckoo's egg tradition is a killer tradition ... When the cuckoo chick grows up, it usually exceeds the size of its foster parents. However the foster parents have so bonded with it ... they are firmly convinced it is their own chick ... The same happens in the Church ... Those with teaching power are often blinded by the long standing and seemingly ancient origins and will seek to defend its authenticity, even though its incongruity is obvious

to impartial observers to it (pp. 5-6) [17].

The current chapter illustrates historically how this defective, misogynist tradition has become the fault line that runs through all theology under the guise of 'dualism', the either/or stance so often taken. Dualism is best explained through the theological dismemberment of women into separated mind and body, a process which has led to the virtual 'disappearance' of women faced with the construct of the 'normal'. The shadow of Eve, as the mythical cause of the incursion of sin into the world, doomed all women to be considered as either virgins or as prostitutes whose only use was for male sexual gratification. Hence the only function for a married woman was procreation, as the following will illustrate.

The defective, misogynist, tradition in the first Millennium

Some of the ideas were first handed down in the first five centuries by the early Fathers of the Church are presented below[18]:

- 'why is man said to be in the image of God and woman is not? ... the image is rather to do with authority, and this only the man has... , while she is subjected to him for he is subjected to no one, as God said "Your inclination shall be for your husband and he shall rule over you" *(Genesis 3:6).'* (John Chrysostom (347-407), Archbishop of Constantinople, scholar and an early Byzantine Liturgist)

- 'Woman is the gateway of the devil, the path of wickedness.' (331 AD, from Jerome, a highly considered Doctor of the Church, the first translator of the Bible into Latin, the

---

[17] Another example of this cuckoo's egg tradition is slavery, to which the non-ordination of women has been compared. (See Wijngaards, 2001,Ch. 2 for a full account of the hold the slavery tradition had over the Church).
[18] Radford Ruether, Rosemary, ed. *Religion and Sexism: Misogynism and Virginal Feminism in the Fathers of the Church,* Simon and Shuster, New York (1974: 150-183))

Vulgate)

- St. Augustine (345-430) who lived in the African Province of the church in Alexandria, and was honoured as a great Latin philosopher and theologian, sincerely believed that women were equal to men spiritually but were subordinate to men in their physical nature and were inferior to men in all other aspects of their lives, including marriage. Although Augustine insisted that celibacy was the higher and better choice, celibate women were still subordinate to men in all aspects of the life of the Church and subject to the authority of male priests, bishops etc. He taught that true women do not question their place of silence and submission to higher male authority and that sex, although necessary for pro-creation, was always 'sinful'. The tragedy is that Augustine's erroneous teachings on women, sex and procreation have shaped Christianity till the present time, as many of the remarks CWO have heard on the Piazza of Westminster from both Roman Catholics and Anglicans, testify: 'no menstruating women on the altar.'

In spite of these strictures, in the first 1,000 years of the Church, inequality was far less evident than later. Empresses, as well as Emperors, called for and attended the early Councils of the Church. Women as well as men were in charge of double monasteries and there is now a well- researched tradition on women as Deacons (see www.wijngaardsinstitute.org). This practice was not confined to the Eastern part of the Church, which during this time was the centre of Christianity, but also occurred in the western part of Christendom which endured and survived the 'Dark Ages'. There is also a tradition found on women's tombstones which offers proof there were women presbyters during these times[19]. (See the work of Professor Otranto

---

[19] The following books are essential reading for the understanding of the role of women *Deacons and Priests in the First Millennium*: John Wijngaards (2002) *The Women Deacons of the Early Church* (Norwich:

and Mary Ann Rossi).[20]

Second Millennium (1000–1500):
the gradual rise of the centralisation of the papacy

At the beginning of this era, communication was difficult, so few people knew much about the papacy and its role, but the advent of the second millennium was to witness the gradual growth of the power and centralisation of the papacy, especially during the reign of Pope Innocent III (1118-1216). This change was the direct result of the historical shift in the rise of towns, especially in Northern Italy, and initiated the rise of Universities in cities such as Bologna, where early Canon Law emerged. It is difficult to get a real feel of a period which was so exciting for those who lived then. At the same time as the centralisation was taking hold there was great intellectual creativity. This led to the beginnings of different schools of theological thought and many spiritual initiatives by both women and men.

One of these schools derived from the theology of St Thomas Aquinas O.P. (1225-1274), who later became known as the 'angelic doctor' of the church though he was less famous in his own time. One important aspect of his thought was his adherence to the tradition of Augustine on woman; thus he united the patristic thinking of the church fathers with medieval thought. To quote but one example of many from Aquinas: 'Woman was created to be man's helpmate, but her unique role is in conception ... since for all other purposes man would be

---

Canterbury Press); John Wijngaards (2001) *No Women in Holy Orders?: The Ordination of Women in the Catholic Church: Unmasking a Cuckoo's Egg Tradition* (London: Darton Longman & Todd).

[20] Professor Otranto and Mary Ann Rossi found important historical material in the Vatican archives as well as on tombstones making it clear that both women deacons and presbyters existed in the early church. See *Journal of Feminist Studies in Religion, article by Mary Ann Rossi* and the film produced by Angela Tilby Nov.11th. 1992, *The Hidden Tradition.*Further information in werbsite www.vfa.us/Mary_Ann_Rossihtm.

better assisted by other men' (Ruether1974: 213-266).[21] Even the well-known 11th century St Bernard of Clairvaux,nicknamed 'golden mouth', along with others described women as 'a bag of shit' ! (Grace Jansen, 1995:132)[22]. We should always remember that these writers were men of their time, highly influenced by the feudal religious cultures and the lack of scientific knowledge. However, whatever the merits of their other words, they must now be recognised also as channels of the misogynist tradition.

It was during this period, in 1215, at the Third Lateran Council, in the papacy of Innocent III, that the Church began its call for the celibacy of all clergy, following the example of monastic celibacy.[23] However, it took until the 16th Century at the Council of Trent (see below) for the Church to make the celibacy of the priesthood a central part of its reform of the Church.

---

[21] The chapter by Eleanor Commo McLaughlen in Ruether's book from which this is quoted is entitled, 'Equality of souls, Inequality of sexes: Women in Medieval Theology.' She gives a detailed understanding of the problems inherent in Medieval Theology, suggesting 'that it was human sexuality itself, not primarily the woman, that was feared by the monk. Homosexuality was more of a daily threat to the chastity of the monk than the seduction of a beautiful woman. Could the frequent outcries against the dangerous female be a projection of that fear of the implications of friendship among the brothers?'

[22] Grace Jantzen, Power Gender and Christian Mysticism, (Cambridge University Press, 1995).

[23] A powerful one woman play, All That I am by Irene Mahoney,O.S.U., (Private Publication)speculates about what happened to the women who were discarded by their priestly husbands when the decree on celibacy became Church Law. Mahoney also includes two other well-known characters: St Augustine's mistress and Dietrich Bonhoeffer's fiancée to whom he was engaged only three months before his imprisonment. The play gives voice to these women, discarded by their partners, with the words 'And What About Me?' The whole play is written as The First Epistle of Sarah, named as the wife of Simon Peter. This important but little known play was performed by Roberta Nobleman at the first Women's Synod in Gmunden, 1996, using scripture, music, mime and masks.

In spite of this theologically based verbal abuse, the spirit of women was not dampened. Their desire for the new was ever present. For example the rise of the wandering Friars, the Franciscans and Dominicans, in the 13th and 14th centuries, attracted so many women who wished to follow this way of life of preaching and teaching, that the Church responded by enforcing 'Enclosure Laws' on 14th and 15th century women religious. The psychological effect of enclosure resulted in what is known as the '15th century 'golden age of mysticism', an explosion of women visionaries. Some of these visionaries are occasionally referred to as the 'battered wives of the Church'. As these women were denied any active expression for their inner power, this power exploded vertically in inner visions. It was a psychological release of frustrated spiritual and physical energies.

Medieval women were very creative in their ways of outwitting Church control. Their visions became a source of power and a way to gain the respect of the Church. Hildegard of Bingen, 11th century, is one of the earliest well known examples of these women, but there are many more[24]. Another significant phenomenon is the rise of the Beguines in the early 13th century; these women initially wanted to be free from Church control, an enterprise in which they succeeded for nearly 200 years. Matthew Paris, the chronicler of the time, was so impressed by them that he placed them alongside the Friars and even claimed that Beguines were better known than the Friars.

In 13th century Milan a completely new phenomenon occurred, described as the rise of a female incarnation of the Holy Spirit. She was called Gugliema and her followers became known as Guglielmites. This movement grew out of the discontent with the condition of the Church in Milan, especially with the dispute that was taking place over the election of the next Archbishop. The aim of the Guglielmites was to establish a female church and cardinals. They

---

[24] Walker-Bynum, Carol (1994), *Jesus as Mother:Studies in the Spirituality of the Higher Middle Ages;* a shortened version is available in Poole Ch.2. (Canterbury Press, 2001).

claimed that only with the advent of a female church would worldwide salvation be possible. They were not a large group and ended with the death of Gugliema in 1274[25].

One of the most remarkable women of the 14th and 15th century was Christine de Pisan, a well-educated woman from a wealthy background, born in Venice around 1400. She lost both her father and her husband at the age of twenty-five. She was left with three children and the accumulated debts of both her husband and father. She is known as the first professional woman writer and was able to support herself and her family by writing. She was so depressed over all the negativity written about women that she became the first woman to take on the tradition from her own experience. Her famous work, 'Querelle de Femmes', began a three hundred years intellectual debate on the battle of the sexes. Christine discovered that the first task of any woman setting out on a career of her own was to prove her own humanity and her capacity for thought, since women were not considered to have the necessary faculties for education and personal thought. The intellectual life was the preserve of men alone. Women's only real use was for childbearing, as indicated by Thomas Aquinas (quoted above), and as they were continually reminded. From the 16th century onwards, the struggle of women was to get access to education which at this time could only be obtained through two avenues, convent or court.[26]

---

[25] 1978 *Studies in Eccelsiastical History-Subsidia I, (* The Ecclesistical History Society *I* by Blackwell: Oxford)..

[26] Malone, Mary T., *Women and Christianity*, vol.3 (2003): *From the Reformation to the 21st century*, Chapter 2, p.14. Vol. I of her trilogy is *The First 1000 years* (2001), and Vol. *2* is *From AD 1000 to the Reformation* (2002). All are published by the Columba Press, Blackrock, Co. Dublin.

The Reformation and Counter Reformation 1500 – 1750

The Council of Trent -1545-1563

The Renaissance, a period that encompassed also the Reformation, was a time of great turbulence and disquiet as new ideas were broached and discussed. It was a time of re-awakening of civilisation after the torpor and laxity of the end of the medieval period. The Church faced its greatest crisis with the laxity of the Popes (the infamous Borgias), Archbishops, Bishops and clergy in general. Yet despite, or perhaps because of, a greater degree of turbulence than churches and society had previously faced, women became a major preoccupation of religious leaders, philosophers and politicians. The 'Querelle de Femmes' continued throughout The Council of Trent (1545-1563)[27], the reforming council of the Church. All aspects of Church teachings were covered, most of the decisions reached remaining until the present day; the central task however was the reform of a decadent clergy, including Popes, Archbishops and Bishops, and the setting up of seminaries. It had proved impossible to implement clerical celibacy. Paul III (1534- 1549), who opened this

---

[27] Trento was a free city in Italy of the then Holy Roman Empire. It was the German capital of the Prince Bishopric of Trent. Although the Council lasted eight years, in fact, it only met for about four years, in three sessions and during the reigns of three different Popes, Paul III, Julius III and Pius IV. Political and religious disagreements among its members and beyond were the cause of the intermittency of its sessions, which numbered 25 in all. It began with only 30 Bishops attending but gradually grew to 255. The Popes did not attend the Council meetings and were represented by their Legates who knew their views. Its purpose was twofold, to define the doctrines of the Church in reply to the heresies of the Protestants and to bring about a thorough reform of the inner life of the Church. Briefly the following topics were covered: Scripture, Tradition, Original Sin, Justification by Faith, Sacraments, the Eucharist and the veneration of Saints (H.J.Schroeder O.P. *The Canons and Decrees of the Council of Trent* (Tan Books and Publishers, Inc., Rockford, Illinois, 1978).

Council, was himself the father of two illegitimate children and had several grandchildren; he was a reluctant reformer but had to draw on the riches of the reforming element of the Church, those who had remained faithful to the biblical and mystical tradition, the Beguines, the Mendicants and the founders of religious orders. The search for high quality priests had plagued the Church for centuries. The rot was everywhere; some priests did not even know the words of absolution, while their concubines had long abounded in parish records.

Nothing was gained for women at this Council. It is also sad to realize that the major reformers of the 16th century, Luther or Calvin, did little to change the treatment of women: Luther could write, "If a woman grows tired of childbearing and dies from child bearing it matters not. Let her die from bearing, she is there to do it.' It is because of this lack of change in women's position in the Renaissance and Reformation that the 20th century feminist historian, Joan Kelly, raised the question 'Did women have a Renaissance?'[28] It was not until the 17th century Quakers, founded by George and Margaret Fox, that there was any beginning to the repudiation of the traditional ideas about women; they insisted that it was not the will of God that women were inferior to men. To this day, many people who once belonged to some form of institutional religion have sought and still seek refuge with the Quakers, when they have found their former religious allegiance too oppressive.

The witch hunts 1560-1760

It is in the witch hunts (often referred to as the 'holocaust' of women) which lasted from the latter part of the 15th century till well into the 18th century (1560- 1760), that the full horrors of this myth-based understanding of women reached its climax. Inevitably, the ones who suffered the most were the very poorest women in society. The

---

[28] Joan Kelly, *Women, History and Theory: The Essays of Joan Kelly* (Series Women in Culture and Society, 1986)

Malleus Maleficarum (1484) is probably the most despicable document ever written in the name of the Church. The Pope commissioned two Dominicans, Kramer and Sprenger, to deal with the matter, and this document rapidly flourished in 19 editions. It sprang from an epidemic of sexual anxiety sweeping through Germany because men were becoming impotent and women unable to conceive. The blame was laid on women, just as the blame of original sin was laid on Eve, by declaring that some women were having sex with the devil. Although the witch craze did not get thoroughly going until the 16th century, during the Reformation, there was a foretaste in Germany of what was to come: thousands of women and children (considered children of the devil) were tortured and slaughtered and several German villages were left with no women and children.

Thanks to *The Crucible* by Arthur Miller, about the Witches of Salem and based in Protestant New England, USA, twentieth century theatre goers were alerted to this past horrific phenomenon. However, recent women historians, especially Anne LLewellyn Barstow in *Witchcraze: A New History of the European Witch Hunts in European History* (1994), has now unearthed accounts illustrating how widespread this enforcement was in Europe. Barstow, working from historical records, estimates that over three hundred thousand women were burned to death up to 1760. This estimate does not include those who either died under torture or were murdered in prison.

The following is but one example from Bavaria to show how random was the choice for burning women as so-called witches in the 16th century. The young Duke, Maximilian of Bavaria, after an intensive Jesuit education, became concerned about witchcraft. His wife could not conceive and he feared the curse had been put on his family. He called for a witch hunt; one of the chosen families to bear his wrath was the Pappenheimers. The story is horrific. Anna, 59 years of age with seven children, was the daughter of a grave digger and the wife of an itinerant privy cleaner. The jobs were despised and the people were treated as outcasts. The parents and the two adult children were arrested and brought to trial. Anna, as a woman, was considered particularly guilty and after repeated torture confessed to the usual accepted form of witch behaviour - night flying, sex with demon lovers, murdering children to make ointments from their bodies, and accepting the devil's orders. The entire family was convicted of witchcraft and thousands gathered to watch: 'The worst dimension was the stripping of the four so they could be burned with hot pincers and then the cutting off of Anne's breasts. Pieces of her breast were forced into Anne's mouth and into the mouths of her two adult children, while the younger children were forced to watch. The eventual burning, several hours later, following more torture (Barstow 1994:143-145). Church bells were rung and the ecclesiastical dignities watching these events were dressed in their finest garb. It is not surprising there was no further unrest in Bavaria. The terms mass murder, holocaust, or ethnic cleansing can all be applied to this 'reign of terror' for women. [29]

In spite of this terrible treatment of women during the Counter Reformation of the later 16th – 17th century some great women saints arose who tried to defy the last decree of the Council of Trent, which was the continuation of strict enclosure for women religious. This enforcement had remained for many reasons and fitted the inherited norms of the time, one of which was to prevent the sexual scandals that had abounded in Renaissance times, something which had provided Protestant reformers with a great deal of ammunition for the Reformation. To work actively among the people was therefore closed to women religious. The following were some of the outstanding women who were called to challenge the church's attitude to them and all women.

---

[29] It is horrific to know that in the rural villages of Papua New Guinea, it is still common place for women to be tortured and killed as witches. Now, at least, the local Archbishops are speaking out about them. (*Tablet* 23 Feb. 2013 p.29).

Three women stand out in the 16th century as radical reformers, Angela Merici, founder of the Ursuline Order in 1530, Mary Ward, founder of the English Ladies, also known as the 'galloping girls'(now the Company of Jesus), and Teresa of Avila, who began her re-founding and reform of the Carmelite tradition in 1554. Angela Merici, founded one of the most innovative groups of women in 1530 in Brescia, northern Italy, calling her order the Ursulines. She saw the need for women to minister to other women who were in great poverty. She circumvented the requirement of enclosure by insisting that her members were all voluntary. Most lived in their own homes and were poor, at least for the first 100 years. The older women looked after the younger women as they ministered to the poverty of other women around them, and some preached. But as the years went on the freedom of the Ursulines from local Church control was gradually eroded, and enclosure was enforced on them for over 300 years. Mary Ward another great innovator, founded her Congregation at St. Omer, France. Mary was convinced that God wanted the women of her group to take on a similar character, intention and work to that of Jesuit men. What the Jesuits, the great reforming congregation of the Reformation, did for young men, she wanted to do for young women. She even believed that Papal approval would be given to her ideas; instead, in this form her congregation was suppressed. She was totally ahead of her time and fearless in the extreme in pursuit of her calling. One of her famous sayings was that 'in time women will do great things'.

Angela Merici and Mary Ward were inspired by similar visions of what women could and should do in the Church. Similarly, after her conversion in 1554, Teresa of Avila felt herself not simply to be called to the contemplative life but also to reform it. Her vision owed little to the Council of Trent and she too was to suffer greatly from the curtailment of her activities as she moved from Convent to Convent. St John of the Cross, who was younger than her, was her spiritual director. Two other women of the 17th century were also partnered by like-minded clerics: Jeanne Chantal, who worked with Francis De

Sales, founded the Visitation sisters, and Louise de Marillac, who worked with Vincent de Paul, founded the Sisters of Charity. It is interesting to note that by this time women's visions alone were no longer sufficient for them to gain influence in the Church; they now also required a spiritual director who was sympathetic to their vision.

The Age of Enlightenment – 18th century

In the 18th century Enlightenment period, often named the 'Age of Reason', the 'man' (literally) of reason was considered the highest form of humanity against whom all others had to be compared. This period fed directly into the French Revolution of the late 18th century and reached its climax in its replacement of all religion with the worship of reason. The first protests of the revolution were led by women, who were seeking bread for their families; however the revolution soon descended into violence against all sections of society. The rumbling of the 'tumbrils' has been well documented in books and films. The women who had initially joined in the call for 'liberty, equality and fraternity' and had believed that they too were included in the movement were rapidly disillusioned. Salons led by wealthy, educated women, where many of the ideas of the revolution had been discussed, were all closed down and many of these influential aristocratic women ended up at the scaffold. One of the best known is Madame Roland, who cried out on the scaffold, 'Oh, Liberty what crimes are committed in thy name' (Poole 2001:28). Women gained nothing from the revolution but it was a consciousness raising exercise which was to develop into the suffrage movement of the 19th and the feminist movement of the 20th and 21st centuries.

It is interesting to note that the greatest degree of women's religious creativity in the Church was the founding of 400 female Religious Congregations in the early part the 19th century, and for the first time attracting mainly poor uneducated women. Many were now called Papal Congregations, meaning that they were not dependent on the local Bishop. At the time this status was emancipatory, enabling these congregations to spread freely over the world for the education of girls and women, and to provide nursing care for the sick. These two options were the only careers open to women at the time; a vast missionary movement spread rapidly to Britain, North America and Australia and later to many developing countries. This development in women's religious life can, in hindsight, now be understood as an important step in the development of women's awareness of the control that the Church had over their lives.

The Papacy and Women: The Marian Age (1860 – 1960)

In spite of the creativity displayed earlier by   founders of Religious Congregations, together with the secular rise of the suffrage movement, the mid 19th century also witnessed the rise of a Marian Age and a new Mariology. At this time Britain was in the forefront of the Industrial Revolution; the sufferings and displacements of the majority of the population, from the country to factories and the accompanying sweated labour in the rising new towns initiated a similar phenomenon in parts of Western Europe, the USA, Australia and New Zealand. Its other effect was the rise of wealthy industrialists. Birmingham was a good example of this: the wealthy moved out of the town to the country, where their wives formed the basis of a Romantic middle and upper class movement that began to redefine women's role as being in the home as loving caring wives.

Meanwhile during all this disruption of people's lives there was a series of Marian apparitions that led to an increase in Marian exaltations for almost a century. For example the 'miraculous medal' devotion arose out of the visions of Our Lady to Catherine de Laboure, a Vincentian Sister, in Paris in 1830. In like manner in 1858 the 'lady of the visions' of St Bernadette of Lourdes identified herself as 'The Immaculate Conception'. This set the seal on the Dogma of the 'Immaculate Conception' that was defined in 1854 by Pius IX. Other important apparitions were to follow: Knock, in Ireland 1879 and Fatima in Portugal 1917. All these devotions continue unabated today, but the Declaration of the Assumption in 1950 by Pius XII can be seen as a kind of 'bookend' putting a closure to this period of sustained Marian exultation.

Many Church leaders interpreted the Marian century as a triumph for a certain Catholic vision of women: the triumph of the historical male dualistic vision of humanity into two very different species, a dominant male and a 'uniquely glorified' female. Mary Malone claims: 'Post-revolutionary Europe fell in love with the feminine ideal of sweetness, delicacy, refinement and virtue. For the Catholic Church, the new feminine provided a counterforce to the world of men. As men began to abandon the Church, during the French Revolution, the Church gradually became feminised. The Protestant model was created from the same ingredients, but was provided with a larger range of options' (2003:205).

Out of this model came extreme role reversals. Men were now painted as 'violent beasts'who could not control themselves at the sight of a woman. Women lost their negative role as harlots and Jezebels and now became the guardians of the morals of society, taking all the burden of caring morality on their shoulders. In addition, as men began to adopt a more casual attitude towards the church, it was asserted that women were more susceptible to the Christian message than men. Women now became perceived as more Christ-like than men and the ideal imitators of Christ in their ability to bear suffering, their patience and their silent invisible struggles, an image repeated as recently as 1988 in John Paul II's encyclical, *Mulieris Dignitatem* (see below).

The interpretation of the Marian visions in this way has led to so much misunderstanding of the fullness of female humanity. Mary, in sexless, disembodied purity, presents a totally unattainable model for women. However, in the 20th and 21st centuries, many female theologians, musicians and poets are reclaiming the true tradition of Mary as a strong, gentle, priestly woman, who is no unattainable model but a creature of flesh and blood who suffered as we all do from the stresses and strains of living. Many women found and still find a real devotion to Mary outside the Catholic concept of the 'glorification' complex of the Church. There is another theological Marian tradition emerging in the rediscovery of Mary for a modern age (Chapter 5).

Mary's significance is that she was full of grace and from this we can begin to recover a renewed appreciation of the grace that suffuses all creation with God's love and endows all nature with 'sacramental significance'. From this can be derived the possibility of developing an ecclesiology from the tradition of Mary and the many dogmas that now surround her (Tina Beattie, *The Tablet* 21st Jan. 2013:15)

From the Declaration of Infallibility (1870) to Vatican II in the 1960s

The story of the Church and women is now taken up again through the declarations of the various Popes in the 19th and 20th centuries. Pius IX (1846 - Feb. 1878) - the longest reigning Pope in history, so far, 32 years in all - was a man of violent mood swings who was fearful of the growing democratic freedoms of the 19th century. He particularly feared losing his power in Italy with the increasing demand for the unification of the nation, and that the Italian army would encroach on the Papal States. He knew this situation would diminish the political power of the Papacy and consequently issued *The Syllabus of Errors* in 1864. In this he condemned liberalism, socialism, democracy and freedom of thought, education, press and religion as modern errors. In 1870 his fears were realised with the Unification of Italy.

Pius IX had already called the Bishops together in 1869 to what is now known as the First Vatican Council, and in 1870 the Infallibility of the Papal Magisterium in faith and morals was declared. When it was clear that the more moderate tone of the document was not to be the final version, some sixty of these minority Bishops left Rome under protest rather than attend the fourth and final session of the Council. The results of this Declaration were widespread, especially in the British Church, which was still very much in its infancy, only having been re-established in 1852. Cardinal Wiseman became the first British Cardinal to be appointed to this re-established Church, which soon fell under the spell of the 'ultramontane' (literally from 'over the Alps') theology and this led to the thorough Romanisation of the British Church, something which was to shape it until Vatican II in the 1960s. Some British Catholics did try to save the inherited tradition of a more localised Church; one of these was Bishop Alexander Goss of Liverpool (1856-1872), who prophesied that after the Decree of Vatican I, the bishops would degenerate into 'satraps dispatched to the Provinces', or *'puppets of the papacy' (Adrian Hastings* (1986:147).

The founding of the English College in Rome, the Venerabile, which was to become the main training ground for the future episcopacy of this country, engendered the permeation though all seminary life of the ideal of being 'more Roman than the Romans. This growing centralisation of the Church fed on the 'Marian' social construct of what a woman should be and together these two strands gradually affected the hard-fought struggle of the religious founders for greater freedom for women from central Church control. Consequently the word 'anonymous' is written large over anything religious women wrote, and pietistic hagiographies became the characteristic writings of the time. This led to Religious living lives that were parallel to those of other women, something also reflected in different approaches to the 'suffrage' movement of the early 20th century in Britain, which the 'official' Church did not support. In a private paper written for the Sisters of Notre Dame de Namur in 1994, Professor Susan O'Brien traces this loss of the 'cutting edge' of the women's orders back to 1850. Thus, in spite of all the good work they continued to do in the many schools and hospitals they set up, women Religious became trapped, for nearly half a century, in a retrograde church culture.

Nevertheless, because of the considerable influx to this country of those fleeing from the anti-clerical laws of France and Germany,

Convent schools increased in number. Adrian Hastings asserts that 'Very probably, the Church in England had, in proportion to the number of Catholics, more Convent schools than the Church in any other part of the world and the effects of this on religious practice was not inconsiderable' (1986:144). The Code of Canon Law in 1917 was the final nail in the coffin which enshrined limited roles for women in Church law. On the other hand, in spite of the heavy restrictions placed on their way of life and those of women in general, the Sisters in these schools also provided strong role models for girls.

However, the stratification of women's role in the Church did not go unchallenged; the first known Catholic reform movement in Britain, St. Joan's Alliance, was founded in 1911 as a reaction to the suffrage movement. Many educated Catholic women, who were a part of the leadership of the suffrage movement, were the first to raise the possibility of the ordination of women and other social issues for women. So far there has been no research on how Catholic parishes responded to votes for women, though the fact that so many poorer women took part suggests that individual Catholic women may well have been involved. It is known that a Canon of a London church did support the suffrage movement. On the other hand in one Catholic parish, in Poplar, London, those who tried praying for women's suffrage 'were beaten up by the people attending' , (Paula Bartley, 2003: 92).

These changes, together with the developments in ecumenism and the freedom of the 'flapper girls', both in the 1920s, proved all too much for Pope Pius XI. He followed a similar response to Pius IX in the *Syllabus of Errors*, by issuing the decree *Casti Connubii* (*Chaste Wedlock*) *in 1930*, in a response to the Lambeth Anglican Synod's approval of the use of birth control in limited circumstances. The Pope re-stated the official teaching of the Church forbidding any artificial means of birth control as well as abortion but asserting the glories of marriage and the right use of sexuality. In addition to these specific topics, the Encyclical includes the condemnation of 'women's emancipation as undermining the divinely founded subordination of women to male authority, as a deflection from her true role as wife and mother.' Clearly the Church had not realised that working class women, in the Industrial Revolution which started in the 18th century, were the first to go out to work into factories, thus becoming the fodder of the cotton industry, just as third world women and children are cheap fodder for the West now.

Only upper and middle class women had the wealth, through their husbands, to stay at home and fulfil these wifely functions full time. Poor women have always had to do more than one job in order to fill the mouths of their ever growing families. The church today makes claims to be 'the church of the poor', but it has a responsibility of its own in the very teachings that still underscore many of the reasons for women's poverty.

Vatican II – 1962 -1965

Pope John XXIII (1958-1963) could be regarded as something of an aberration, because he let fresh air into the church and declared how much dust had gathered on the seat of Rome since the era of Constantine in the 4th century, when church and state became one. He was widely respected and loved worldwide. In his late 70s, when he came to the Papacy, he was a round, ordinary, very loveable man with a big smile. In both his actions and demeanour he is a role model in the development of a new way of papacy. Pope Francis declared him a saint, alongside Pope John Paul II, in 2014, while Francis's first Apostolic Exhortation, *Evangelii Gaudium,* 2013, can be seen as a return to the Spirit of the openness of Vatican II.

Pope John's call for *aggiornamento,* to bring the Church into the modern world, was above all an attempt to change the 'mentality' of the Church. This desire was expressed, in different degrees, in all the documents of Vatican II but especially in *Gaudium et Spes* which expressed the Joys and Hopes for the Church; lay members of the

Council, including the 24 women who attended the Council[30], had most input in this document.

However, because of the growing call for women's ordination after Vatican II, especially from the Canadian Bishops in the early 1970s, Paul VI set up a Biblical Commission to report to him on the question. Their findings were very interesting. They unanimously agreed by 17 votes to none that the New Testament does not settle the question in a clear way once and for all[31]. In other words, there is nothing in scripture contrary to this idea and it should be opened up for wide discussion by the 'people of God'. Even after the research of the Biblical Commission, Paul issued on 27th January 1977 *Inter Insigniores* which stated that the matter was closed: women can never be priests because they cannot be 'icons' of Christ. This was clearly illustrated in the most recent Code of Canon Law in 1983, where women's experience was not taken into account, reiterating the Code of 1917, in Canon 1024, 'Ordination is restricted to baptised men' (Ida Raming et al., 1993:56).

It is important to notice that women were not involved in any deliberation on this topic as though they were non-people with no minds or experiences of their own. For the loyal women of the Council, the 1977 decree *Inter Insigniores* was the final straw. Rosemary Goldie, one of the 24 women observers at Vatican II and a great favourite of Paul VI, in her reflections on what happened after Vatican II, spoke of the growing disillusion and mistrust after hopes had been so raised at the Council. The immediate era after Vatican II was a very important stage in the development of feminist theology, followed closely by the awakening of women's consciousness on a wider scale than ever before, as illustrated in Chapter I.

---

[30] Mc Enroy, Carmel, *Guests in their own House: The Women of Vatican II* (New York: Cross roads, New York, 1099).

[31] To read a fuller account of this Biblical Commission see www.wijngaardsinstitute.org website. It is very informative and worth a deeper understanding of this very tricky problem.

However, in spite of the development of the Movement for the Ordination of Women in the Anglican Church, parts of that Church were no further advanced at this time. In 1978, at the Anglican General Synod, Bishop Graham Leonard cited his understanding of the Anglican headship theory, "I believe that ... Christ was incarnate as a male ... not because of social conditioning, but because in the ordination of creation headship and authority is symbolically and fundamentally associated with maleness'. The Anglican Church did not vote for women priests till Nov 11th 1992 and then with the modification of the so-called 'two integrities ' out of which came 'flying Bishops' for those parishes that would not accept women priests. Or as one Anglican priest said: 'We burned them once so we can burn them again'. He condemned himself in his own words.

In 1984 there was an exchange of four letters between Archbishop Runcie of Canterbury and Pope John Paul II on the question of women's ordination. These letters are important as they sum up the only known internal discussion on this question in the Catholic Church. This exchange of thoughts on the question of women's ordination took place before the final vote in favour in the Anglican Church. They give a very clear statement of the official teaching of both churches and the reason behind the various documents that were later issued by the Catholic Church. Yet again no women in the Catholic tradition were considered worthy of consultation on this subject.

The first letter came from John Paul II. The Pope acknowledged that a great increase in communion was happening between the two churches, but said that any further discussion on women's ordination would place 'an increasingly serious obstacle to that progress.' It is of note that these very words were used in 1992 on the BBC news, by Vincent Nichols, made Cardinal in 2014; it was his comments that further urged us on to begin CWO. They were used in CWO's first press release - hence the strong ecumenical origin of CWO which continues to this day.

The seven points of Runcie's reply arrived a year later after deep consultation within his own church, 1984 (Malone, 2003:226-236).

1. Those Anglican churches that had already ordained women had done so for 'serious doctrinal reasons'.

2. 'There exists, in scripture and tradition, no fundamental objections, to the ordination of women.' The New Testament by itself alone does not permit a clear statement on this issue.

3. Substantial doctrinal reasons for the ordination of women: 'the fundamental principle of the Christian divine economy of salvation ... the eternal Word assumed our human flesh in order that with the passion, resurrection and ascension of Our Lord Jesus Christ this same humanity might be redeemed and taken up into the life of the triune Godhead.'

4. 'The humanity taken by the Word ... must be inclusive of women, if half the human race is to share in the redemption he won for us on the cross.' The Archbishop of Canterbury is obviously referring here to the ancient Christian formula dating back to the 4th century, *what is not assumed is not redeemed* i.e. if women are not assumed as full human beings then only men are redeemed.

5. The priest is commissioned by the church to represent the whole body of Christ. This 'complete humanity is all the more perfectly expressed in a priesthood open to both women and men.' This is direct opposition to *Inter Insigniores* and the 'icon' argument that because Christ is male therefore priesthood has to be male. But we have to remember that the Catholic Church has not since 1896 considered the Anglican priesthood as valid, and in 2001, Cardinal Kasper, in a talk given at the Anglican Synod in Canterbury made this very clear.

6. Runcie then gives a cultural argument, one that the Catholic

Church does not see as relevant to this issue. The letter continues to state that human societies have accepted the cultural changes on the position of women and as a result 'the representative nature of the ministerial priesthood is weakened by a solely male priesthood.'

7. Runcie says he would have preferred ecumenical agreement on this question and he fervently hopes ecumenical discussion will continue.

The full answer to these questions came from Cardinal Willebrands, rebuffing the Anglican arguments and the result was the subsequent Papal declarations[32].

In 1988 Pope John Paul II returned to the 19th century Marian tradition of the 'glorification' of women 'in *Mulieris Dignitatem*, with the well-known phrase *'women are equal but special,'* nicknamed by many as 'the pedestal peddlers.' This was followed by a stepping up on the non-ordination tradition in 1994: *On Reserving Priestly Ordination to Men Alone, Ordinatio Sacerdotalis*. In this document, John Paul II introduced a new theological term known as 'definitive', one rung below 'infallible', despite the fact that there had been no consultation with bishops before it was issued.

This was followed by the *Responsum* by the then Cardinal Ratzinger, who was head of the Congregation for the Defence of the Faith (the CDF), underlining even further the impossibility of ordaining women, using again the new theological term 'definitive' and claiming that it belongs to the deposit of faith. An outcry followed which led to Joan Chittister OSB writing about what she called the 'Dubious Dubium' because it ushered in a new theological category – 'definitive'. She wrote:

'This document has brought us to the end of "ordinary time". It is the catalyst for change, for it brings us to the pinnacles of insight, of

---

[32] Malone, 2003, :. 230 -236.

what a church should not, as well as what a church should be. A Church at last truly in the image of God: "in our own image let us make them male and female." Only when this Church images God, will we know that God is in this Church.' (A private paper given to CWO members).

The fundamental problem for the Church is that the non-ordination of women is in the wrong theological slot. The right place for this topic lies in the 'social teaching' of the Church, a teaching which mirrors the changes in human societies as society evolves in its understanding of sexuality and creation in order to bring to fruition the words of Christ, 'I have come that they may have life and have it to the full.'

The position did not change during the pontificate of Pope Benedict XVI who made it clear that he wished to purify the Church from the so-called 'dissidents'. The result has been continued silencing and persecution, particularly of theologians, priests, women and men religious and now lay people who dare to challenge any official church teachings on this topic. This situation is now easing under the Pontificate of Pope Francis 2013.- 'I have come that they may have life and have it abundantly ' (10:10)NIV.

Conclusion

This chapter has traced the many somersaults the Church has gone through to keep women away from the altar of God. The arguments against women's ordination in the Church have shifted through the ages, but as the Church was challenged to face the growing question of why women are not ordained, Papal statements became almost hysterical in their rapid and repeated rebuttal of any hope of women's ordination. The methods of the 19th century no longer work in a 20th and 21st century, except for a rapidly decreasing vocal few. The growth of the 'sensus fidelium', i.e. the growing non reception of the magisterium's arguments on this question and others by the 'people of God', is becoming unstoppable.

John XXIII understood this in the 1960s when he stated at the opening of Vatican II how much dust had grown on the See of Peter since the 4th century, when Church and State became one in the Roman Empire. There is a growing desire now in the Church to 'make all things new', especially with the election of Pope Francis (2013). Herein lies the success of Vatican II, the steady growth of the development of the Magisterium of the 'people of God'.

The notion of women, as second class inferior beings, objects of sexual desire and either harlots or virgins still exists today with an often less than subtle modern twist. However, the birth of feminist scripture and theology in the latter part of the 20th century has seen a rapid growth in a feminist, biblical and theological critique of inherited gender and symbolic theories - the 'Great Feminist Awakening' of the 20th and 21st centuries.

Reflections

- Reflect and write down any new facts you did not know before.

- What in this chapter resonates with your experience.?

- How do women overcome their inferior position by their own creativity in the 21st century?

References

Gnanadason, Aruna (1993) *No Longer Secret: The Church and Violence Against Women* (WCC Publications).

Hastings, Adrian (1986)*The History of English Christianity 1920-1985*, London:William Collins

Jantzen, Grace (1995) *Power Gender and Christian Mysticism*, Cambridge: University Press

Kelly, Joan (1986) *Women, History and Theory: The Essays of Joan Kelly* (Women in Culture and Society, Chicago and London: University of Chicago Press

Llewellyn Barstow, Anne (1995) *Witchcraze: A New History of the European Witch Hunts in European History : Our Legacy of Violence Against Women* London: Harper Collins

McEnroy, Carmel (1996) *Guests in their own House, the Women of Vatican II*, New York: Crossroads

Mahoney, Irene OSU (1987) *All That I am.: What About Me?*(Private Publication- play performed at first Women's Synod in Gmunden in 1994).

Malone, Mary (2003) *Women and Christianity: Volume III, From the Reformation to the 21st Century*, Dublin: Columba Press

Poole, Myra (2001) *Prayer, Protest and Power: The Spirituality of Julie Billiart Today*, Norwich: Canterbury Press

Radford Ruether, Rosemary (ed.)(1974) *Religion and Sexism: Images of Women in the Jewish and Christian Traditions* New York: Simon and Schuster

Vander Stichele,(1993) Caroline, Ad van der helm, Bert van Dijk, Rik Torfs, Svetko Veliscek *Disciples and Discipline : European Debate on Human Rights in the Church,* Leuven: Leuven Press

Walker-Bynum, Carol (1994) *Jesus as Mother: Studies in the Spirituality of the High Middle Ages* Berkely/Los Angeles/London: University of California Press,.)

Wijngaards,John (2001)*The Ordination of Women in the Catholic Church: Unmasking a Cuckoo's Egg Tradition,* Norwich: Canterbury Press

*The Revised Standard Version of the Holy Bible, Catholic Edition (*1966 Nelson London.)

Papal Documents

Pius IX   (1864) *The Syllabus of Errors*

             (1870) *Infallibility of the Papal Magisterium in Faith and Morals.*

Pius XI   (1830) *Casti Connubii (Chaste Wedlock).*

John XXIII (1960s)   Vatican II document, *Gaudium et Spes: Pastoral Constitution On The Church In The Modern World.*

John Paul II(1977) *Inter Insigniores*

             (1988) *Mulieris Dignitatem.*

             (1994) *On Reserving Priestly Ordination to Men Alone, Ordinatio Sacerdotalis',*

             (1994)*Responsum* to above by Cardinal Ratzinger.

Francis   (2013)*Evangelii Gaudium*

Articles

Beattie, Tina (2013) *The Tablet* 21st Jan.

Studies in Ecclesiastical History-Subsidia I (1978). published by *The Ecclesiastical History Society I* by Blackwell: Oxford .

Private papers

Chichester, Joan OSB 1994 *The Dubious Dubium*

O'Brien, Susan 1994 *Historical Past- Future Perspective,* given to the Sisters of Notre Dame de Namur

AWAKENING: TO 'SYMBOLIC SHIFTS' IN FEMINIST THEOLOGY

'Until you get man off your eyeball you cannot see anything clearly' [33]

Towards symbolic healing

Alice Walker's famous saying shook the imagination of an earlier generation but it is as relevant today as then. We are nowhere near shaking off these false images. We have all been taught, from our earliest years, to wear 'patriarchal glasses' and have all been conditioned by male-only language and imagery of God in official Church liturgies. This is summed up simply by Mary Daly: 'if God is male, then the male is God' (1975:38).[34] All language, especially 'God language', is metaphor, so if we can only speak to God as a male then we have what is called a dead metaphoric symbol, which becomes idolatry.

One of the best books to read to counteract these ideas of an all-male God and Trinity, is Elizabeth A. Johnson's *She Who Is: The Mystery of God in Feminist Theological Discourse* (1992). In the introduction to *The Elephant in the Room* (2014), Mary Malone describes the effect on her of a talk on the Trinity; she says, ' I am accustomed to closing

---

[33] Walker, Alice (2004) *The Color Purple* (Phoenix, Orion Books LTD.London).

[34]Daly. Mary (1975) *Feminist Post Christian Introduction: The Church and the Second Sex* (New York, Harper and Row), together with her sustained analysis in *Beyond God the Father: Toward a Philosophy of Women's Liberation*. (This edition includes an original reintroduction by the author. Daly wrote her first book in 1968, *The Church and the Second Sex,* as a direct result of Vatican II. The book was a serious exposé of Christian misogyny, especially within the RC Church. It is one of the most important critiques of sexism in the Christian tradition.

down a part of my mind as this kind of discourse happens, but on this occasion, I realised with new certainty that if females are absolutely excluded from this egalitarian and intimate male relationship then the whole metaphor makes absolutely no sense except as an idolatrous concept.'

The purpose of symbols is to take us beyond our 'finite' thinking :'A symbol is a species of sign which carries a fullness of meaning...it introduces us to realms of awareness not usually accessible to discursive thought, giving participatory rather than speculative knowledge.'[35] The question of symbolism is discussed fully later in this chapter when explaining the real meaning of the 'virgin birth' and the question of all language as metaphor. For the purpose of this book the first part of this chapter concentrates on a critique of the sexualised imagery of the ever popular bride and bridegroom typology, followed by a short critique of the understanding of the Eucharist held by the 20th century theologian Hans Von Balthasar. The second part of the chapter concentrates on feminist insights into the role of Mary, since she has a central role in healing the theological defectiveness of the second class tradition of women.

But above all this chapter is underpinned by the fact that the equality argument for women's ordination is far from enough. It is useful as a first stage of awakening but then it is necessary to look into matters at greater depth. Nowhere is the inadequacy of a purely egalitarian perspective better illustrated than in the need for a greater understanding of the importance of redeeming the present, all pervading, patriarchal symbolic system in which we are living and progressing into a more inclusive feminist symbolic understanding.

---

[35] Maeckelberghe Els (1991) *Desperately Seeking Mary* (22) in article by Janet Soskice,

Part One: Sexualisation of 'symbolism' during the second millennium of Christianity

Reference has already been made to the flexibility of Christian thought in the first five centuries of Christianity. In various ways, this flexibility remained throughout the first millennium of Christianity. During the second millennium however, symbolism became gradually more defined in male terms, with the gradual centralisation which has occurred in the Church from the 11th century to the present day.

In her book *New Catholic Feminism: Theology and Theory* (2006), the British theologian, Professor Tina Beattie, has taken up the challenge of re-visiting the symbolic thought of Hans Von Balthasar and his resultant influence on the Eucharistic thinking of the Church.[36]

The Eucharist

Whether they realise it or not, women have to live schizoid lives whenever they go to Mass. God is totally imaged in male language and symbol. The scene is set at the very entrance to the Church as Mass begins with the current all male dominance of priesthood and diaconate. The male priest has been perceived as the main 'God bearer', something which no one can live up to. However, placing women's experience at the centre of theological thinking means that virtually every inherited given comes under scrutiny and is subject to critique, revision and renewal in the interest of greater liberation for the mystery of God.

The bride and bridegroom symbolism

The reasons why only men can be priests has always been based on shifting sands. In the first five centuries, before Church Councils, there was an intimate relationship with the maternal body which was not sexualised. It was used to try to explain the relationship to

---

[36] Beattie's earlier book, *Eve's Advocate* (2002), concentrates on Mary.

each other and to God in complex ways. This means although the analogy of marriage, 'the bride and bridegroom' symbolism, has always been applied to the relationship between Christ and his Church, and since the Middle Ages, between Christ and Mary, it is clear in *Ephesians* 5, where Paul writes about the universal Church and not just the local, that this image does not refer to the sexual relationship but to the life-long principle of self-giving love that makes marriage analogous to the love of Christ for the Church[37]. It is not about the domination of the one over the other, although this is the way in which it has been played out in history, and resurrected theologically as an all-male 'functional symbol' for priesthood, as it is referred to still in the 21st century. (The equivalent of this in some Protestant theology is 'headship' theory.) Paul's teaching is instead about mutuality and right relationship between the one and the other. The male does not take precedence or act as a 'functional' representative or an 'icon' of Christ, just because Christ was born male, because 'all are one in Christ'.

Unfortunately, the subsequent misreading of the scriptures has led to the sexualised symbol gradually infiltrating the mindset of many theologians. Professor Beattie concludes by showing how the effect of this transition on the symbolism of the Mass means that it has gone

---

[37] As with all the Pauline letters, there are continual disputes between scripture scholars of different generations as to how much can be attributed to Paul alone in his letters. What is sure is Paul is a key figure in the gradual maturing in the understanding of the central message of the life, death and the resurrection of Jesus. The *Letter to the Ephesians* needs to be read as a whole to understand Paul's development of the theme of the 'body of Christ' which arises out of the chief concern, which at this time was to counteract Jewish hostility to the new Christian embryonic belief. To this end Paul widens the concept of the 'body of Christ' to an understanding that the scope of salvation is cosmic. In the *Letter to the Galatians* this is extended further in the well-known words: 'There is neither Jew nor Greek, there is neither slave nor free, there is neither male nor female; for you are all one in Christ' (3:28).

from being a celebration of death and rebirth focused to a large extent on the maternal body towards being a celebration of sexual intercourse mainly focused on the male body. The Church now insists on an entirely sexualised account of salvation by the use of narrow scriptural texts and their misreading: 'To argue, that Christ's Eucharistic gift of self is the action of the bridegroom in such a way that its performance requires a male body to make it an act of coitus and not of self-giving in death. The symbolic function of the priesthood is therefore no longer primarily concerned with death but with sex, since both male and female bodies die and therefore either sex could represent the death of Christ' (Beattie 2002: 79-80).

To sum up, in the early middle ages, the focus of the Mass was not just the sacrificial death of Christ, but the incarnation as a whole; it was not till the latter part of the Middle Ages that the Mass came to be understood more as a sacrifice. By 18th century enlightenment period, the 'man of reason' had become the ideal person. Women could not represent Christ on the altar, because Christ's death was that of a perfect human being; women, understood as being defective, were not perfect. In our own age, the female body is recognised by the Church, as 'equal' but 'different', replacing 'defective' with glorification but still having the same overtones. Women are still incapable of representing Christ because 'Christ's kenotic[self-emptying] complete self-giving has become implicitly associated with the male organ, with all the pagan overtones that this implies' (Beattie 2002:80).

The theological and symbolical culmination of this past tradition appears in the 20th century Swiss Catholic theologian Hans Von Balthasar (1908-1988)[38], held in high esteem during the papacies of

---

[38] Hans Von Balthasar was a medical doctor from Switzerland, who was first a Jesuit (1929-1936), but left, and became a Diocesan priest and set up a secular Institute. In 1940 he took on a convert Adrienne Speyr, who was to have a great influence on his writings. She was also a medical doctor but unfortunately was also a hysteric who claimed to be a mystic. Balthasar's

John Paul II and Benedict XVI. In his 'symbolic theology', his 'Theo-drama', Von Balthasar has gone to great lengths to use sexual imagery, especially the bridal imagery of the scriptures, to demonstrate the suitability of the male body to represent Christ as the 'seed' implanted in women. In his Eucharistic thought he takes his erotic male imagery to a startling climax as 'an endless outpouring of his whole person, such as a man can only achieve for a moment with a limited organ in his body'. Beattie writes forcefully on this concept of the 'identification of Christ's death with uniquely male experience of male ejaculation ... Ultimately this means that women have become bystanders in the metaphysical consummation of homosexual love' (2002: 119-120).

It is to be hoped that we are nearing the end of this literal translation of bridal imagery and long held 'defective' and 'different' imagery of women, now that Pope Francis calls for a development of the theology of women. However he is still at the stage of using the term **'functional'** for upholding an all -male symbolic representation of priesthood. In the process, the literal sexual scriptural misreading of the bridal imagery and Eucharist is now being challenged theologically, no matter how uncomfortable and distasteful both the theology and the challenge may make us feel. It is an impossibility simply to add women into this sexualised cultural symbolism on the basis only of equality and morality.

Before leaving this section of the chapter it is interesting to note that St. Therese of Lisieux wrote of her desire to be a priest in her book *The Journey of a Soul* (1898). She stated that she was glad that she was dying at the age of 24, as it was the age at which a man could be ordained as a priest. She was far from alone in this desire at the turn of the 20th century. Added to these desires is the fact that there has always been a long held popular tradition in the Church of seeing

---

aim was to search for an intellectual response to the Western critique of Christianity. His Theo-drama, 60 books in all, contains a violent sexual undercurrent towards female sexuality.

Mary as priest. However, in the light of the gradual growth of female demands for the vote, which the 'official' church was against, the Papacy decided gradually to repress this growing devotion. In 1916 the church officially decreed that pictures of Mary in priestly vestments were forbidden. This was followed in 1927 by the Church forbidding any discussion of this devotion, followed in 1930 by *Casti Connubii*, which condemned all forms of the growing women's liberation movements as not being of God. For the Church, woman's place was in the home. And so began the century when the Church tried to muzzle women and men on topics that it did not agree with, a tactic that has not worked but rather has given rise to more and more discussion.

The question arises as to what new 'symbolic and sacramental possibilities might be revealed if the female body at last acquires priestly, sacramental significance' (Beattie 2002:291). As 'Body Theology' upholds, where we put our bodies matters, symbolising our cultural status. The placing of our bodies on the Piazza of Westminster, for over 20 years, has become a symbol of women who live on the edge of the Church. Women are no longer passive, non-essential bystanders, or merely an audience for the male ritual in what should be the central act of unity in diversity in the Church.

The birth of the Church from the body of Christ is one of the most enduring truths of the Catholic Church, but it is so translated into male terms that it covers, with a symbolic and verbal veil, the wholeness of Christ, and distorts the real meaning behind Christ's death and gift of salvation. This is where searching for the real Mary and the sisterhood between Mary and Eve is essential. The words of Christ on the Cross 'it is consummated' come alive in meditation - we need to dwell on the word 'consummated' and its deep meaning played out in history. For me, it signifies Christ redeeming the world from a patriarchal way of being and thinking, and resurrecting to a scriptural and inclusive way of being. But for new thoughts to take flesh we need to remind ourselves continually of the frequent words of the scripture scholar Schüssler Fiorenza , that we need 'women of courage and men of conscience' .

Part 2: *Genesis* 1-3 and the Annunciation: the sisterhood of Mary and Eve

When we look at the Christian story we need to return to the foundation stones of our understanding of salvation and to work towards a creative re-figuration of the narrative of faith and its symbols in chapters 1-3 of *Genesis*. At the moment the literal, traditional interpretation is that Eve, the woman, brought sin into the world; she has subsequently come to be seen as the representative of all women. The problem is that this is a simple literal translation of a story from another far away culture, an interpretation which has never been corrected by the Church. This is illustrated historically in Chapter 4 of Mary Malone's *The Elephant in the Room* (2014). It is an early symbolic story on the Fall of humanity but it reflects the inherited confusion on the fault line that runs through scripture and history on the so-called role of women. As Christianity develops, women come to be seen not only as the source of mortality but also the source of all evil. Hence women fluctuate from being witches to domestic goddesses until Mary comes along.

It is important to note there is a great difference between the use of language before the Fall in Chapter 1 of *Genesis* and the following two chapters. In *Genesis* I language is used to describe the creation of the world as a means of loving communication between God and humankind, who find that everything created is 'very good'. But after *Genesis* 1 we have two chapters on the Fall. Here the language conveys deception and argument, even arrogance and shame, naming and blaming: '"Have you eaten of the tree of which I commanded you not to eat?" The man said "The woman whom thou gavest to be with me, she gave me the fruit of the tree, and I ate"' (3.3-12). Today people sometimes refer to Adam as a 'wimp' because he does not even acknowledge his own sin, blaming the woman. Eve's reply is different: '"*The serpent beguiled me and I ate*"' (v 13). The truth is that they both shared the blame of the Fall. Both were faced with using their unique human capacity of free will to respond, or not, to the Word of God. The Fall as depicted in the scriptures is the symbol of all other awakenings, personal and societal – the choice between good and evil.

The Annunciation and the Virgin Birth:
'in partu'- the unbroken hymen

When we come to considering the Virgin birth it is important to understand the purpose of religious symbols, among which the Virgin birth is probably one of the most controversial. This is so important that it is worth reminding ourselves of the following definition mentioned at the start of the chapter. The purpose of symbols is to take us beyond our 'finite' thinking: 'A symbol is a species of sign which carries a fullness of meaning ... it introduces us to realms of awareness not usually accessible to discursive thought, giving participatory rather than speculative knowledge.'[39] Symbols cannot be replaced or created at random, they are dynamic, and have various interpretations in different cultures and periods. For Sarah Boss, a modern British authority on Mary, the cult of the Virgin in Western Christianity can only be understood against the background of our changing relationship with nature. For example at the height of Medieval times Mary was perceived as the all-powerful 'Queen of Heaven' at a period when people experienced themselves as dependent on their physical environment; that environment was seen as the bearer of God incarnate, as Mary herself was the bearer of God incarnate. This way of understanding Mary and other saints can be re-echoed in many poor countries today, where the hope of miracles is the only means of cure.

In other words we are dealing with a symbol that has been understood differently according to the dominant culture in which it

---

[39] Maeckelberghe, Else *Desperately Seeking Mary* (1991:22)

has been incarnated. For the western world, Mary's Virginity has been stripped of all meaning, by the finite mind; it is a model which is useless for women if she is understood to have conceived and given birth in a way completely out of the reach and experience of all other women.

It was not till the 2nd century A.D. that the doctrine that Mary was the 'New Eve' emerged as the beginning of Marian theology. We also know that Mary, a Jewish woman whose name Maryam, Miriam, shows her to be a daughter of the Old Covenant as well as the new, a part of the *anawim*, the remnant of the Jews, awaiting, with open minds, for the Messiah for whom they longed. Ruether indicates that the early Latin theology situated Mary's importance around her function of being 'the representative of all humanity in its original goodness This makes Mary the model of the church:...a Marian Spirit filled Church'(16).

It is interesting to note that Beattie criticises the dominant image of Church that emerged in Vatican II i.e. the 'people of God'. The weakness of this image, for her, is that it has downplayed the maternal element of Mary, as understood in scripture and the early Church, and blocked the vision of a Marian/spirit filled Church.

In *God's Mother, Eve's Advocate* (2002) Beattie develops much of her symbolic theology from the work of the 20th century French women psycholinguistic analysts, in particular the thought of Luce Irigaray[40].

---

[40] Luce Irigaray, Julia Kristeva and Helene Cixous are three of the most influential French writers on women and symbolism. Despite their differences, the question of language predominates in all their thought on symbolism and theory. This is true particularly in Helene Cixous, who sees women's ways of writing as different from male forms. These psycholinguistic authors are difficult to read and for a full understanding demand concentrated study of their works. But they have been used by Tina Beattie and others as a way of expressing their own theological thoughts. (See Lisa Isherwood & Dorothea McEwan (eds.) *An A-Z of*

The central theme of all Irigaray's work is to explore the marginal space that women hold in the symbolic order. Irigaray also finds gender difference encoded within the very structure of language, not just the individual words. Irigaray names this 'la lange' to indicate that it has a broader context than that of words alone. La Lange refers to the encoded male structure of all language.

The Annunciation as a 'symbolic' interpretation of the relationship between Eve and Mary

The importance of Beattie's interpretation is that it is a 'symbolic approach.' Her aim is for a symbolic reconciliation between Mary and Eve using many different tools of human and biblical expression, poetry, art etc. Beattie accepts that her approach requires 'nimbleness of mind' to make different disconcerting connections between apparently non-related religious symbols. In re-defining the symbol of the Annunciation, the unbroken hymen of Mary's virginity, she clears the ground for her theology by first dismissing the well-known 'penis envy' theory of Freud, who claimed that women wished to be male and possess male penises. As a product of a patriarchal culture. Beattie understands that if we want to change the world we must first change the way we speak and think about the world in the many facets of our lives. It is like turning ourselves inside out and unlearning the many religious myths we have been taught. All this is part of often uncomfortable personal awakenings that can disorientate us for a time, until this new thought begins to inhabit both our minds and the way we act. These awakenings are part of Christ's prophecy that he would *make all things new'*, a process that begins within us.

Beattie places her emphasis on Irigaray's theory of 'la lange', the male structure of language that encapsulates any thought, but points out where she differs from Irigaray in the development of her symbolic

---

Femininst Theology (Sheffield Press, 1996: 72-73) and, in more detail, Moi, Toril (ed.) *French FemininstThought: A Reader* (Oxford: Blackwell, 1993).

theology. From the psycholinguistic perspective, Beattie claims that to understand Mary as both a virgin and mother, the central Christian task, is to liberate language from its dualisms - either/ors - which is the way the 'fallen world' of our daily reality has been constructed. Beattie concludes that the concept of virginal motherhood is not a denial of the goodness of human sexuality but 'an affirmation that in Christ opposites are reconciled without loss or distinction' (2002:125). This need to reconcile opposites, the central message of the Annunciation, can be found in many attempts of the early Fathers of the Church to find a language to express this unity in difference. Beattie notes too that Cardinal Newman, in the 19th century, also defined the notion of Mary as the 'daughter of Eve unfallen' as being more faithful to some aspects of patristic thought than the later idea that Mary's perfection stands as a condemnation of Eve (2002:148).

As women have always been downgraded in society and religion, women's collectively discerned experience, as a basis of theology, is the beginning of de-stabilising the neo-orthodox religious tradition of what it means to be human, with its faulty historical anthropology. This degradation of God's creation, described in the Bible as 'good' also relates to the experience of lesbian, gay and transgendered people, whose experience is also crucial in the building of a new religious anthropology. 'What does it mean to be fully human?' is one of the crucial questions of the 21st century.

Thus one of the first things to be achieved is to liberate Eve from being understood as the cause of all the sins of the flesh. If women are perceived in scripture as the main cause of sin, in the Annunciation, women with Mary are the first to receive the redemption of her Son. Mary is a central figure in the liberation of all, but especially women, who are made holy in flesh and word. Mary's virginity is a symbol of life, not death. Her acceptance of her full personhood, as the Holy Spirit hovers over her, leads to her freely chosen 'fiat', her 'yes'. This is Mary's great awakening as to the uniqueness of her calling.

Elizabeth Johnson, in *Truly Our Sister: a theology of Mary in the Communion of Saints* (2003) puts flesh on the meaning of the symbol of virginity: 'Virginity indicates a state of mind characterised by fearlessness and independence of purpose', whatever one's choices in life, married or not. Virginity is to retain our inner autonomy, living by our own centre that only grows stronger as we get older. It signifies that a woman is not defined by her relationship with men. It is a quality of religious commitment and denotes an openness to the Spirit of God'. '(2003:30-31).

Elizabeth Johnson calls the emphasis on motherhood one of the cul-de-sacs in the understanding of the real Mary[41]. The development towards a distinct personhood for women beyond biological factors is still a work in progress, but essential if women are to be theologically included in any priestly role in the Church and have their own distinctive relationship with the divinity identified.

The Magnificat (Mary's Prayer *Lk.* 1:46-55) is a wonderful charter for women but it needs to be understood beyond a socio-economic presentation of the salvation of the poor, important as that is. The Magnificat does not idolise the poor but lifts Mary and all women into a personal relationship with the Divine. They become distinct human and divine subjects, with boundaries of their own being, capable of their own good and evil. The language of this canticle makes clear that divine love is particularly on the side of those whose dignity must be recovered, and it resonates deeply in the ears of Christian women: 'he raises the lowly and the rich he sends empty away'

---

[41] The poetry and writings of the great American writer Adrienne Rich are very illuminating on the subject of Motherhood, see *Of Woman Born: Motherhood as Experience and Institution* (London: W.W. Norton, 10th edition, 1995). All her writings are worth reading – she was so in advance of her times and her poetry is some of the finest of any time. A truly gifted woman.

Historical symbols of Mary

The customs of the Church were not built in a vacuum and starting from the 4th century many of the early images of Mary were based on those of previous female deities - woods, trees, lakes, pilgrimages etc. The iconography of Mary seated with her child on her lap looking outward is patterned on the pose of Isis with Horus, while the Black Madonnas of Le Puy, Montserrat, Chartres and elsewhere derive from the ancient black stones connected with the fertility power of earth goddesses, 'black being the beneficent colour of subterranean and uterine fecundity' (Johnson, 2003: 75). The Council of Ephesus (431) gives the same evidence of mingling pre-Christian times with the formative years of Christianity. As soon as Mary was claimed as God-bearer, *Theotokos*, the crowds proclaimed *Great is the Diana of the Ephesians* (Acts 19:23-24).

Johnson writes of the many cul-de-sacs to which this symbolic Mariology has led us. In medieval times there was a great growth in devotions to Mary together with speculation on Mary herself. One of the most powerful images was that of Mary as Mediatrix (Mediator) of All Graces, derived from the writings of theologian Peter Damian who wrote: 'Just as the Son of God has deigned to descend to us through Jesus, so we must also come to Him through you' (Johnson 2003:120). From this image the Cistercian monk, St. Bernard of Clairvaux, visualised Mary as the compassionate 'go-between', in the shape of the 'neck', between an angry and unforgiving God who needed to be placated. Mary became the all compassionate caring mother who was to intercede for us with a very severe father, who needed to be 'softened up' to forgive all his erring children. While Jesus Christ was acknowledged as gracious Saviour, the increasing juridical penitential system led to the sense that his role as judge superseded his mercy. It is no wonder devotion spread to Mary who began to take the place of the Holy Spirit: 'We have a picture of a vigorous Mariology growing ... in an impoverished theological garden' (2003:123).

By the 16th century attributes from the Trinity were assimilated into Mary's image and she often appeared more God-like than God. As the Catholic tradition developed after the Reformation, the priority of God and the centrality of Christ were made officially clear. However there was still plenty of space to attribute to Mary important functions, and for visions of Mary to become more important. This culminated in the 'mariology' of 19th and early 20th centuries and two very important dogmas. The first was from the vision of St. Bernadette at Lourdes, where Mary revealed to Bernadette that she, Mary, was 'The Immaculate Conception' (the belief held that Mary herself was conceived without sin), followed in 1950 by the dogma of the Assumption (that Mary was assumed body and soul into heaven when she died). These two dogmas have subsequently been interpreted as follows by those wishing to see them in a broader context:

1. 'The Immaculate Conception' was not just about Mary but signifies that God gives Grace to all freely.

2. 'The Assumption' meant that we as individuals will be perfected by God.

The US Catholic Bishops offered this interpretative key – that these two dogmas were not 'isolated privileges but mysteries filled with meaning for the whole Church.'

Mary and Vatican II

The question of Mary's rightful place in the Church, inside or outside, caused the most bitter controversy of the whole Council. The discussions arose out of *Lumen Gentium: The Constitution on the Church*. The Bishops of Germany, England, France, Belgium and Holland favoured the more biblical and theologically rigorous approach, of the first millennium (minimalist) and therefore wanted Mary to be within the Church document. The Spanish, Polish and Italian Bishops followed the maximalist approach to Mary of the second millennium, that Mary should stand alone outside *Lumen*

Gentium. On October 29th 1963, the vote was finally taken. It was the closest vote of the Council, with 1,114 votes in favour of incorporating the Marian teaching into the last chapter of the schema, and 1,074 against.

Pope Paul VI was not always happy with the outcome of the schema, but ten years after the Council, realising that devotion to Mary was waning, he wrote an apostolic letter entitled *Marialis Cultus,* the Cult of Mary. He set out four important principles, based on the Council's findings, to be the basis of any future Marian devotions: biblical, liturgical, ecumenical and anthropological. In paragraph 37 of the letter, he states that the traditional piety of the submissive woman is now repellent to most people. Paragraph 36 is even more interesting; he states that 'cultural norms are not eternal: the Church does not bind herself to any particular expression of an individual cultural epoch or the particular anthropological ideas underlying such expressions'(133). Unfortunately, John Paul II did not follow this view in *Mulieris Dignitatem* in 1988. Instead the image of the 'ideal face of woman' emerged.

Johnson also critiques, on two accounts, some of the post Vatican II writings of people like Congar, Schillebeeckx and Boff, especially the idea of Mary as the maternal or feminine face of God: 1. It blocks the possibility for women of their 'full identification with the divine image and likeness' 2. 'God does not have a feminine or masculine face'. However, in the ecumenical spirit of Vatican II some Catholic theologians paid particular attention to Protestant critics who claimed that Mary's role had been substituted for that of the Holy Spirit. This is a theme returned to in the latter part of this chapter. However, Johnson does accept that the many images of Mary reveal 'how theomorphic women actually are', being able to represent so many aspects of the Godhead (2003:91).

Miriam the Jewish Woman

The growing critique of the inadequacies of the symbolic concept of

Mary has led historians and theologians to go beyond the transcendent images of Mary of the second millennium to an imagined historical Mary – *Maryam* – Miriam, the Jewish woman. Johnson does this in the latter part of her book and more recently it is pursued by Mary Athans in *Quest of the Jewish Mary* (2013)[42]. There is little about Mary in the Bible so we have to rely to a large extent on retrieving the human woman from the history of the time. We do know that she was a dark haired Jewish woman who spoke the Aramaic language of the peasant class with a Galilean accent and lived at the birth of the first thousand years of Christianity with all the problems of that period. Mary was married to Joseph, a widower, a man considerably older than herself. We also know that with Joseph she brought up a large family, not the cosy image of the threesome of the Holy Family. The question of 'the brothers and the sisters' mentioned in the Bible has long been contested. The other children could have been children from the previous marriage of Joseph, they could have been Joseph and Mary's own children (James is later called the brother of Jesus) or other close cousins. The latter is the present teaching of the Church but the matter is far from clear (Johnson 2003:195).

We know that Joseph was a carpenter and they lived in Nazareth, in Lower Galilee, a village so poor and insignificant that it rarely appeared in the maps of the time. They came from the peasant class and would have lived in a typical two room house with a roof made of

---

[42]Athans, Mary Christine BVM (2013*) Quest of the Jewish Mary': the Mother of Jesus in History, Theology, and Spirituality'* (, Orbis books, Maryknoll, New York). Readers who would like to delve deeper in discoveries about the Jewish Mary and the customs of her time would find this book informative. It is comparatively short, and reader friendly, supplying many insights Into the customs of the time and illuminating Jewish customs, such as the essential purity pools for both rich and poor. It also describes the essential and high profile roles played by women in local synagogues (2013: 98, 115-19, 135). This book also includes a devotional approach to Mary through the use of the Ignatian *Spiritual Exercises*.

reeds, around a compound in which all the daily living, gossip and village meetings would take place, including all Jewish worship. These spaces of community gatherings were the synagogues of the time. Mary would have had a strong body and psyche, given the daily manual monotonous hard work she shared with all the women of her village. She was a strong, resilient woman, who with Joseph and her family lived according to all the Jewish laws and festivals of her day, listening to the Torah and participating in the Shabbat prayers in all the regular local community synagogue assemblies. The latter were not necessarily buildings but an assembly of the people anywhere they could meet – a home, round a tree, in a village compound etc. The synagogues in poor villages were similar to a modern community centre.

Bernadette Brooten has examined synagogue excavations dating from 27 BC to approximately the 6th century, looking at Greek and Latin inscriptions, from Italy, Asia Minor, Egypt and Palestine, which have revealed the many leadership roles women played in synagogues. She also concludes that women were not seated in an area separate from the men, as dictated by 19th century customs. In modern terms sexism does not seem to have played any significant part in Jewish worship – men and women moved freely within it especially in the poorer villages (Athans, 2013:115-119).

Another myth to be expunged is that of Mary's painless childbirth. She suffered all the pains, blood and gore of giving birth, as all women do. She was a woman of the poor, a migrant, surrounded by wealthy cities and continual warfare. Giving birth is the greatest creative act of all human actions – how much more so for Mary, who gave birth to the Saviour of the world. She is no timid, passive spectator. Mary embraced life as she embraced the message of the angel.

Joseph was far from insignificant in this marriage. He brought the wisdom of his life's experience and the quiet inner strength that goes with it. Given the very fragile and violent times in which they lived

Joseph is a model of gentleness and non –violence. Our imaginations need to bring to life this man: Joseph who protected and loved Mary and all his family so much. As far as we know Joseph and Mary were only married for twelve years as no more is heard of him after the incident in the Temple (Luke 2:41-52). It is presumed that by the age of 30 or before, Mary was a widow, but remained at the centre of the growing Jesus community and was present with them in the Upper Room after his death and well beyond.

Mary through South American eyes

Before we leave this discussion on Mary, it is helpful to widen our vision beyond a European perspective. Just as the Holy Spirit was replaced by Mary in the Middle Ages we find this re-echoed in South American Hispanic theologians in their insights into popular religious practices, including visions of Mary. However, there is a wide diversity of interpretations among them especially that of the well-known vision of Our Lady of Guadaloupe. Virgil Elizondo advances the thesis that the origin of the 16th century devotion to Our Lady of Guadaloupe involved resistance by a conquered native people not only to the European invaders but also to the all-male God in whose name they conquered. In the process of this resistance, the poor and vanquished people became the recipients of a major disclosure in the development of the Christian understanding of God, that the mystery of God embraces both male and female identities. Consequently this living Marian symbol has significance not just for Mexicans, Indians and South Americans, but for the whole Church: it liberates everyone from a restrictive, masculinized view of God' (Johnson 2003:203).

The place of this 16th century apparition was the site of an ancient temple dedicated to Tonantzin, the Indian virgin mother of the gods of pagan times. The dark skin of the woman of the apparition, the language she spoke, the colours she wore and the heavenly symbols that surrounded her were all reminiscent of the goddess of the defeated people. Yet it was not Tonantzin who appeared but the Virgin mother of the Christian God. Elizondo interprets the creative result of this cross cultural encounter thus. Our Lady of Guadaloupe combined the Indian female expression of God, which the Spanish had tried to wipe out as diabolical, with the Spanish male expression of God, which the Indians found incomprehensible, since everything that is perfect in their culture had a male *and* female component: 'Here the male Father God of militaristic and patriarchal Christianity is united to the female Mother of God (Tonantzin) ... which allows the original heart and face of Christianity to shine forth i.e. compassion, understanding, tenderness and healing' (2003: 83). This revelation came at a time when the conquerors were violently killing others as 'pagans'. What came out of this was the birth of a new Christian reality, a new humanity, a new Church. This is no longer an exterminator God but one of goodness and harmony, a God who is on the side of the poor. The Virgin becomes a living locus of the compassionate God in female form.

Another Hispanic theologian, Orlando Espin, offers a different interpretation but keeps the connection with divinity. He questions whether the Church's insistence that this is a Marian apparition is really the 'sensus fidelium' (the accepted, received understanding of faith) of everyday people. He suggests that instead of an experience of Mary, what we have here is a 'superbly inculturated experience of the Holy Spirit' (2003:84). He is not implying that Mary is the Holy Spirit or that Mary of Nazareth appeared in Indian guise. It is not the Jewish woman, Miriam, whom Latinos venerate in this apparition, as there is a notable lack of reference to the Mary of the gospels in this apparition. It is rather the Holy Spirit, translated into a colonial Mexican context to be the reconciling Creator Spirit. Too much talking of the Holy Spirit, at this time, would have fuelled the hostility of the Inquisition. Espin concludes that what we have here is not Mariology but pneumatology, i.e. a revelation of the Holy Spirit, in an 'unexpected and brilliantly achieved cultural mediation' (2003:83), revealing 'the capacity to represent God not only as nurturing, but also as a powerful creating-redeeming–saving God' (2003:86)

The subversive and Spirit-filled Mary

The praying of the Rosary, often dismissed as an unsophisticated way to pray, can be a subversive feminist prayer which illuminates the whole story of Redemption as revealed by Mary's understanding of her mission and life, and as prayed in her Magnificat. Women know that Mary has had special graces but also that she is one of them in the Communion of Saints. Mary of the Third Millennium is no longer outside the Church but deeply rooted within it. There is still considerable research to be done until we understand more clearly the full discipleship of Mary and her development as a model of the Church, or indeed what a Marian Church would look like. Mary's social and historical location places her as a woman of her time but she is timeless in perfecting the fullness of human ability to live a life fully in the Spirit. Mary was as subversive as her Son, and like Mary, women can do the same to give birth to new healthier visions of Church 'where all can lay their heads'.

Conclusion

So we have traced a beginning of the renewal of the understanding of important symbols in the Church: the present scriptural interpretation of the 'bride and bridegroom' image; the Eucharist as understood by Hans Von Balthasar; and a beginning to the retrieval of Mary. All symbols can be made fruitful for a modern, educated age, a work on which our scripture scholars and theologians are now embarked. The riches of the tradition are being re- excavated and brought to public eye by women from different experiences, cultural settings and traditions. To quote Sojourner Truth, the great American black woman of the suffrage and U.S civil rights movement, who lived until she was in her 90s: 'if men can turn the world wrong side up surely women together can turn the world right side up again'.

Reflections
- Are you shocked by the Eucharistic theology of Hans Von Balthazar? Why?

- Language and Symbols: what has struck you most in this chapter on the importance of a deeper understanding of both these aspects of religion?

- Has this chapter helped you towards a renewed understanding of Mary's role in the salvation of Eve and women?

Bibliography
Beattie, Tina (2002) *Eve's Advocate,* London: Routledge

Beattie, Tina (2006) *New Catholic Feminism: Theology and Theory* London: Routledge

Isherwood, Lisa & McEwan, Dorothea (Eds.) (1996) *An A-Z of Femininst Theology,* Sheffield: Academic Press

Johnson, Elizabeth (1992) *She Who Is* New York: Crossroad

Johnson, Elizabeth (2003) *Truly Our Sister: a theology of Mary in the Communion of Saints,* New York: Continuum

Maeckelberghe, Els (1991) *Desperately Seeking Mary: A Feminist Appropriation of a Traditional Religious Symbol* Kampen (Netherlands): Kok Pharos.

Malone, Mary (2014) *The Elephant in the Church: A Woman's Tract for our Times* Dublin: Columba Press

Moi, Toril (1996) (ed.) *French Femininst Thought: A Reader* Oxford: Blackwell

Schüssler Fiorenza, Elisabeth (1983) *In Memory of Her: A Feminist Theological Reconstruction of Christian Origins,* New York: Crossroad

Schussler Fiorenza, (1992) *But She Said: Feminist Practices of Biblical Interpretation* Beacon Press,Boston USA.

Papal documents

Pope Paul VI (1974) *Marialis Cultus*

Pope John Paul II (1988) *Mulieris Dignitatem*

Chapter 6
AWAKENING:
TO NEW VISIONS OF CHURCH

This book has been dedicated to the various processes of change and the pain and 'self-emptying' required during the process of church renewal. The whole book is intended to be a contribution towards an understanding of a Feminist Ecclesiology from a down-top perspective (rather than the traditional patriarchal top-down direction of the church.) This is a quest initiated by an essential question: Who and What is Church?

All attempts to try to envision a new way of being Church can only be aspirational and seemingly utopian, because we are in the realms of the mystery of God. However, this chapter is an attempt to begin to articulate a renewed Church through the eyes of women's experience of oppression. Moreover, there is an increasing understanding by men of how they have been collaborators, maybe unwittingly, in the continuation of this oppression. They too have to undergo a time of pain and letting go, but with words of consolation from Elizabeth Johnson that 'the more feminist you become, the more orthodox your position'[43].

Father Aloysius Pieris S.J., a Sri Lankan theologian, reminds us that we are not in for an easy ride when we dare to challenge a process of renewal rather than simply a reformed Catholic Church. 'Reform' he says, 'is smooth, renewal is stormy,' and 'Christ came to 'renew' the

---

[43] Zagano. P. & Tilley. W.T, (1999) (ed.) *Essays on the Theology of Elizabeth Johnson,* New York: Crossroad

face of the earth'. (*Give Vatican II a Chance*, 2010)[44] This is his continual theme throughout the book.

Reform was the favoured word in the early stages of the critique of the Church in the early 20th century. However, 'renew' became the watchword after the 'aggiornamento' of Vatican II, i.e. opening the Church to the world in the 1960s. The previous chapter, on 'Symbolism', has indicated the depth of renewed understanding required of the Church's Religious Symbolism. The Church has to delve deeply into the richness of the Christian past of the first two millennia in order to enrich the third millennium, in which we now live. The Covenant God made in the Old Testament was to free the slaves from Egypt, a symbol for all oppressions and injustices, in whatever guise they may manifest themselves. A thorough renewal will take time until a renewed linguistic and symbolic theology begins to take hold of both our spirituality and our theology. However, for any lasting, fruitful renewal the listening process has to be two-way between the edges and the centre.

The Blue Print model of Church

The three essential attributes of Church are: the Institutional, the Mystical and the Prophetic. When one of these aspects dominates, the other two come in as correctives. This is what has happened since Vatican I. Since the promulgation of 'the Infallibility of the Papacy' in 1870, the Institutional aspect has grown out of all proportion. As pointed out in Chapter 4, prior to that date many people did not even know a papacy existed. Who could have foreseen that the process of the gradual centralisation of the papacy, begun in the 11th and 12th century, would have ended up in the understanding of the Church as

---

[44] Aloysius Pieris S.J. has long been one of the leading Asian theologians, who lives in Sri Lanka. He is not only as a great scholar of Christianity but also as a scholar of other religions, especially Buddhism. *'Give Vatican II a Chance: Yes to Incessant Renewal, No to Reform of the Reforms'*: Sri Lanka:Tulana Jubilee Pub. 2010.

unchangeable in its hierarchical Institutional model of the Church?

Post-modern age

Modern ecclesiologists all write clearly about the dangers of this inherited 'Blue Print' model of Church: this all-prevailing model is under severe criticism today. Lieven Boeve from Leuven University, Belgium, states: 'The Church has been left somewhat in limbo since Vatican II and still awaits an energizing ecclesiological vision for the future' (in ed. Mannion, 2007:ix)[45] He goes on to stress the serious dangers inherent in this all-pervading model, concluding, 'only traditions that acknowledge their own limitations and specificity ... are worthy of any claims of legitimacy' (2007: 101)

In this post- modern, pluralistic age our leading ecclesiologists believe we can no longer live within one single tradition and that there is an imperative for us to think and act ecumenically. Roger Haight S.J, one of the most distinguished ecclesiologists of the 21st century, writes in the third Volume of his *Christian Community in History* [46] that 'The Church really cannot be understood apart from the world in which it participates' (2008: 223). He concludes that 'salvation does not lie in the Church but in the world' (2008: 233-269). This does not mean Catholics have to take on an inferiority complex but they have to get rid of any feelings of superiority. The concept of having models of the Church is the thinking of the past. The call today is to use our imaginations to re-envision what a just and inclusive Church might look like. This will confront us all with the deep cultural prejudices we have inculcated, and in this way renewal will slowly

---

[45] Mannion , Gerard (2007) *Ecclesiolgy and Postmodernity: Questions for Our Time,* Minnesota: Liturgical Press (a Michael Glazier book)

[46] Roger Haight's three Volumes constitute one of the most comprehensive and scholarly works on how the Church and all churches have been understood through the ages. He moves beyond history, especially in the third volume, *Ecclesial Existence: Christian Community in History, Volume III, London:* Continuum, 2008. In this volume he probes the essence of the Church in all its diversity.

take hold.

What is emerging is the need for a more durable, transferable, flexible ecclesiology that is always pastorally/praxis (i.e. practice) orientated and is more self-critical and reflective. The human fear of criticising the hierarchical Magisterium of the Church has pervaded the majority of its members because of the heavy penalties meted out to those who dare to raise their voices in public. Excommunication, the modern version of 'off with their heads!', as the Red Queen says to Lewis Carroll's Alice, is the weapon used on people who are seen to deviate from the thinking of this Magisterium. Hopefully, this atmosphere of fear will gradually evaporate during the Papacy of Pope Francis, and remain so during all future Papacies.

Professional theologians have to be allowed to explore responsibly but freely; there must be no more threats of excommunication and silencing of anyone over such issues as women priests and homosexuality. We need an 'Open Church' with open minds, able to discuss, change and modify opinions to ensure they are of the Spirit. Many people, women in particular, are leaving this Church, no longer able to live two lives: their real lives as thinking adults and the childish inferior position the Church forces them to inhabit.

Feedback from CWO supporters.

There are common themes that run through all the replies that we invited from CWO members. It is not surprising that the word 'inclusive' dominates every reply, as women have felt excluded for so long in the male pantomime, which the all-male Mass has a tendency to become. This problem is not a women problem, it is an all-Church problem, but especially a clerical problem. There is a healthy diversity of ideas amongst CWO members, but a general agreement that can be summed up in the words of Katharine: 'A Church where gifts are shared ... and in the words of an Iona hymn, 'for everyone a place at the table ...', a church where no one has to take a back seat or hide in the shadows because they are gay, lesbian, divorced, disabled - to name but a few'. Sue adds to this reflections of her Iona ecumenical experience as follows: 'My ideal church ... would preferably be where people sit in a round or horseshoe, where there was an open table so that those who wished to take communion could do so ... there would be no in group or out group but there would be an expectation that communicants signed up to an adult course of theological education ... based on scripture and the experiential approach based on Feminist Theology.'

Amanda explicitly raises the problem of the new translation of the Missal as being not only in very exclusive, male language, but also 'verbose and unwieldy and inaccessible': to which Pat adds emphatically, the Church must be 'inclusive at every level especially language.'

Michael takes up the understanding that salvation is in the world not in the Church, and continues the theme of ecumenical priority, plus a world faith mindset:

'Jesus wanted us all to be one ... Not just Catholics, Anglicans, Muslims, Hindus – everyone ... God wants us to know and love our neighbour ... not necessarily go to Mass per se – Mass is just a nice familiar routine ... You get programmed into the habit of getting out of bed and going to Church. I am not saying it is wrong to go to weekly or daily Mass, but it is not the only way to get to know Jesus. Consecrated buildings are useful in some ways, but they are not the real answer ... Yes I love going to Mass ... but it is not the total thing.'

It is not surprising that the question of the present position of women is a high priority and there is a radical questioning of clericalism. For example, Amanda raises the question of persistent 'blood taboos', referred to in the experiences described in Chapter 1 : 'Is the blood flowing from women too close to the imagery of a suffering and bleeding Christ for celibate men? ... It is extraordinary that within our lifetime women were still going to Church to be cleansed after childbirth.' Amanda also raises the question of the redistribution of the wealth of the Church, as does Camilla, who, in her vision of Church, would like the Vatican to become 'the biggest homeless shelter and orphanage in the world. It will have the world's largest free hospital and school. Our commitment to the poor will be at the centre of our faith in a very literal and tangible way'. Pope Francis is beginning to call and act according to Camilla's vision of 'the Church of the poor, the people's church', by his care of the homeless on the Piazza of St Peter's, Rome.

Pat wants a Church locally involved in justice issues, a 'sanctuary for victims of domestic violence, asylum seekers and refugees, all those shunned by society'. Two members want the Church to get 'back to basics', making comparisons with John Major's policy as Tory Prime Minister (1990-1997), adding 'it would be hoped it would be more successful than that doomed exercise.'

A prevailing theme is the de-clericalisation of the hierarchical power of the Church from Rome down to all diocesan and local levels. These ideas include the following: the priesthood does not have to be for life; local communities could choose their own leaders: women and men, married or unmarried, and those with a variety of sexual orientations.

All responses include a dislike of the new translation of the Mass and the way it has been imposed on people without consultation. While all replies recognise the need for leadership, they emphasise that the leaders must be 'well trained, articulate and compassionate', as expressed by one of our older members, Ianthe. Others question the relevance of the word priesthood and prefer the word diaconate, while yet others prefer the word ministry to cover all forms of service. Ruth does not want to see a priestless Church, but says that this priesthood must be much more varied: 'I think there will remain a place for priests, who are celibate from choice, whether they are female or male, but they should not be considered of a higher order than non celibates. Nor do I think a priest must necessarily function as a priest for life ... The ordination could be for life, but the manner of living out that ordination could change according to life circumstances. Also there could be a place for what used to be called "worker priests" i.e. people who have a career or job in another field, but who are ordained as priests, and can act as such in a part time capacity.' In the Anglican Church these people are known as 'non-stipendiary'.

Derek, one of the founding priests of ACTA, states 'I believe that if the Church has a future – and faith tells me it has – then it will have to be a much more evangelical church. Smaller communities without a priest will become normal. They will celebrate together; when a priest is available, this will be the Eucharist, though it may be possible to ordain members of small communities to preside at the Eucharist regularly, to avoid priests dropping in to preside in a number of communities.'

Seminary training comes under close scrutiny, understood by many as 'cultural breeding houses for the Blue-Print. Church'. Members see the present seminaries as very unhealthy training places for future Church leaders. Most believe that their major training should be in the community, with periods away for prolonged prayer, and that all theological training should be in Universities. This should include a thorough understanding of Catholic Feminist Theology, as well as Ecumenical Feminist Theology as a seed-ground for a present and future Church. Above all, priesthood should be judged not by validity or function, a notion still propagated by the Magisterium teachings, but by human fruitfulness.

There is no doubt that the present theology of priesthood has to be dragged out of its patriarchal context. The gender question is not easy and it demands a deep change of consciousness for us all. In religious terms the Church is being called to a radical conversion, a time in the wilderness such as Moses and the Jews had to experience. This will be a time that requires true humility in recognising the depth of the culturised sin we have inherited, which CWO calls the 'sin of sexism', that has been destroying the life of the Church for so long.

The Church has to re-find its moral basis. The days of ecclesiastical courts are over. It is being called to account by the secular courts, including the United Nations. It can no longer hide behind special exemptions and the secrecy of the 'boy's club'. The official Magisterium has proved to be unable to correct itself. The worldwide paedophilia crisis witnesses to that. The quests for changes are growing both from within the Church and outside it and are gathering apace, to show up the present inadequacies as Church.

By far the biggest movement for change, at present, in the Church in Britain, are the concerns of the growing 'listening and dialogue groups' arising across the United Kingdom in A Call To Action (ACTA). This was begun in October 2012, by seven priests, now often referred to as the 'magnificent seven', and is rapidly spreading throughout the UK. ACTA is now in every diocese of England and Wales. The aim is to dialogue with local Bishops. If Pope Francis is able to develop collegiality among the Bishops (which means decentralising the Church so that Bishops and their people can dialogue with Rome rather than Rome deciding everything) and then expand collegiality to every aspect of the Church's life, the people in these ACTA groups and other affiliated groups may well form a basis to assist the Pope's desire for deep renewal.

The aim of this book is to open up discussion and to help people re-think what they believe and why. Karl Rahner S.J. talked of the 'diaspora', smaller groups of Christians scattered round the world, as the future church. Desmond Murphy in *A Return to Spirit: After the Mythic Church* (1997)[47] uses the theology of Rahner and others to

---

[47] This book is an original and convincing analysis of the vast changes taking place in the Church as seen through the lens of Transpersonal Psychology. Father Desmond Murphy is a registered psychologist who has both practised himself, and trained counsellors. The book, aimed at the

explain some of the difficulties we face in coping with change. He takes his knowledge of Transpersonal Psychology as the basis for his book. He claims that this can only flourish when a person is secure in their 'core construct', that is, secure in who they are, and in their experience of God as the underlying essence of their lives. Such people have generally undergone many inner changes themselves and consequently have developed a new world and religious view which has become deeply integrated into their lives. Only when we have a real sense of self can we transcend. (1997: 81 & 83-84).

Pippa has discussed in her chapters the gradual development of new insights and the pain that generally goes with them – 'Loss and Gain' – or as Rita Brock describes it in *Journeys by Heart*, 'the church that has both nurtured and wounded me'[48].

Most liminal boundary conversions are less dramatic than that of St. Paul, generally developing through individual personal awakenings in daily life and then a search for like- minded people with whom it is possible to share.

Seedbeds for renewal and change understood through Transpersonal Psychology

CWO is an example of a female and male group, ecumenically based

---

general reader, does not 'knock' the Church or former generations of Christians; it acknowledges that we cannot blame others who went before us because they lacked the knowledge of our time. It does not deny the conditioning and core construct of people but acknowledges that the Mythic Church or Blue Print Church as we would now call it, has for many people been the vehicle of an authentic personal relationship with the Divine. But Murphy acknowledges that it is less easy to understand those who have the knowledge now but are still blinded by their conditioning and the core construct that results in this split between knowledge and action.

[48] Brock. Rita Natasha (1988) *Journeys by Heart: A Christology of Erotic Power,* New York: Crossroad

from the beginning. Together these groups find their personal thoughts are coalescing. The seedbed for change for the Anglicans was the Movement for the Ordination of Women (MOW). The experiences within these groups are gradually producing individuals that Murphy calls Transpersonal People, the 'seedbeds' of the future. I would include all the genuine renewal groups, national and international, as some form of 'seedbeds' of the future. There are individuals often but not always deriving from these groups, who have undergone severe criticism from the Magisterium even excommunication. This then raises the question: have all Catholics the same personal identity, or are we in transition to replace the 'one size fits all' format? There are an increasing number of people who think the Catholic Church, in its present Institutional form has little future.

However, Richard Rohr wrote the following in his *Daily Meditation* (Feb. 19, 2015) as a timely reminder: 'By definition, the prophet has to be on the edge of the inside of institutional religion. It's a hard position to hold, and it must be held both structurally and personally, with wisdom and grace. There are many times it would be easier to leave the system ... Jesus understood this. He loved and respected his Jewish religion, yet he pushed the envelope wide open. He often healed people on the Sabbath, which was a deliberate statement against making a practice into a dogma that was higher than human need (*Matthew* 12:1-8). Yet he honoured the same Jewish establishment by telling some he had healed to 'go show yourselves to the priests' (*Luke* 17-14). Jesus walked the thin line of a true prophet ... or the central principle, transcend and include.'

The understanding of the psychological development of human beings has undergone a revolution with the development of psychology in all its forms and the necessity of going through each developmental stage for ordinary human well-being. Desmond Murphy writes of Transpersonal Psychology in the same vein. He lists each stage of religious development in the following way: from magic to mythic, to rational independent thinking, and then moving into trans-law. He places 'mythic religion' as appropriate to a child between the ages of seven and eleven, a time when we humans are most vulnerable and our thinking is very literal and concrete. This is where the patriarchal symbols of religion get embedded, when we are taught that religious authority is always right and we should not contradict it. He also acknowledges that many adult people may be well educated in the secular sphere but have remained childish and vulnerable in the religious sphere. However, it is important to remember that we all have bits of each stage within us though one will predominate in the end. None of us ever reach total maturity; we are all in the process of struggling to become mature and will continue to do so into eternity (1997: 51-81).

As the former structural and familiar props are falling away, we all have gradually to face the religious conditioning in our lives and the 'core construct' in our personalities that prefers the familiarity of the past to the challenge of the future. The present popularity of meditation groups, and 'Silence in the City' in London, is a sign that people are looking beyond institutional religion in their search for their personal, immanent God. No doubt this deeper prayer life is a pre-condition in preparing the way of the Lord for a renewed coming. 'Follow me'' are the words of now and the future and many of us will be taken to places 'where we would rather not go'(*John* 21:18), or as Eleanor Roosevelt wrote in the time of the great depression in the USA in the 1930s, we will all be called 'to do the things we think we cannot do'.

Murphy stresses that it is very important to distinguish between trans-law and counter-law people. The former energise and work for transformation, the latter de-energise and are often too angry, who react rather than transform (1997:186-191). The trans-law approach does not reject the past but appreciates its riches. These are not the Pharisees of religion, who put burdens on people's backs that they cannot bear, but as trans-law people, they know, in conscience, when a law has to be broken for the greater good.

Murphy also stresses the difference between surface change, just moving the same furniture around the room, and transformation: 'Future expressions of the Church will not merely dress up present archetypal values in new words and forms. This would be a case of surface structure translation, not transformation. Each age brings new insights into the truth. Succeeding generations can access deeper, less concrete, more abstract, and more universal dimensions of reality. Therefore the future Church (rational- individuated) will express archetypal values that the human race is only beginning to access, for example environmentalism, the population issue, feminism (all indicative of rational – individuation), as well as those that have not been accessed but which the race will need for its on-going evolution ... The future will bring forth other such values and it will be for the Church to embody them. In addition, newer dimensions of abstractness and universalism, which are not immediately apparent in present values will be discovered, and will continually call for integration' (1997:195).

More interesting still and perhaps more controversially, Murphy sees the Western world as more significant than developing countries in this radical transformation, at least as far as religion is concerned in the 20th and 21st centuries. He states clearly that the Church must not place its hopes on the numbers in the developing countries, as a sign of the future hope of the Church, as this is just surface change. He writes: 'The Church sees the Western church as in decline and has turned to developing countries, where Catholicism flourishes, as the wave of the future ... The problem is, what happens when the developing countries reach the same scientific and educational level, as the West, in greater numbers? Their religion will go the same way as the West, unless the West shows that religion can advance to a higher stage. To this extent, the argument about numbers is an indication of surface structure translation rather than transformation.' He says that this approach is sad as it canonises mythic religion as the ultimate and it is contrary to the rights of Western Catholics: 'They have a right to take the next step in religious development of the human race ... the Church is currently failing God, itself and society. The West is also being denied its right and duty to trail blaze the next level of Christian development, by the Euro-centric, mythic power structure of Rome' (1997: 183-4).

Conclusion

As already stated, any ecclesiology is an aspirational undertaking. Many of the above personal visions from our CWO members of what a renewed Church might look like may well sound like Utopia, but what is amazing is the way that so many of these visions, arising from experience, coalesce in less sophisticated ways with those of the leading ecclesiologists of our times. Roger Haight S.J., already mentioned, refers to the Church today as being in a 'Transdenominational Reformation'. Lieven Boeve from Leuven University in Belgium has been concentrating on the development of the local Pauline (small grace-filled missionary) Churches, so long neglected. Karl Rahner S.J, the great theologian of Vatican II, introduced the idea of the 'caesura', a cut or different direction from the past. This theme prevails now as an ecclesiology of 'interruption'; an ecclesiology that has to hold both continuity and change in tension: the development of a theology from 'below' rather than from 'above'.

Little has as yet been written directly on ecclesiology by women, but their insights are beginning to emerge. In the earlier chapter on Mary, reference was made to the Marian Church, with Mary being seen as the prototype of church because of her faith. What is crucial now is balancing the Petrine hierarchical Church with the Pauline local church, the concept of the Marian Church and Karl Rahner's view of Church as a 'virtue Church'. All these ideas need much more thought and understanding through discussion.

Serious recent thinking on the role of the Papacy not only in the

Church but ecumenically was begun during the Papacy of John Paul II in the document known as *Ut Unum Sint* (*That All Should be One*, August 1999). This document reveals that John Paul II was becoming aware, through ecumenical dialogue, that there was some legitimate critique of the authority structures of the Church. The Church, now in dialogue with others, has to begin to lessen its hold, gradually let go of its fears, and drop the inquisitorial techniques of silencing and threatening excommunication, in order to grow into a more mature stance of dialogue as a way of being a living pluralistic Christian community. Mutual listening, dialogue and a process of reconciliation and forgiveness are at the heart of Church renewal.

But above all, if we are called to be a part of the privileged process of re-articulating a meaningful Christianity for a new age, we need to burn with the love of God, until we can say like St. Paul, 'not I but Christ lives in me' (*Galatians* 2:20).

Caritas Christi Urget Nos *–The Love of Christ compels us forward*

Reflections

Consider insights that have come to you through this chapter:

- Where is their resonance with your experience? Where is their resistance?

- Do you agree with Desmond Murphy's comments on the importance of the European Church?

- Reflect on your reactions and why.

Bibliography

Brock, Rita Natasha (1988) *Journeys by Heart: A Christology of Erotic Power*, New York: Crossroad

Haight, Roger SJ (2008) *Ecclesial Existence: Christian Community in History, Volume III*, London: Continuum

Mannion, Gerald (2007) *Ecclesiology and Postmodernity: Questions for Our Time* Minnesota: Liturgical Press, a Michael Glazier Book

Murphy, Desmond (1997) *A Return to Spirit: After the Mythic Church*, Basingstoke: Gill and Macmillan.

Pieris, Aloysius S.J.(2010) *Give Vatican II a Chance* (Tulana Jubilee Publications.)

Zagano, P. & Tilley, W.T, (eds.) (1997) *Essays on the Theology of Elizabeth Johnson*, New York: Crossroad

Bible version New International Version

Our CWO LOGO of 3 spirals in a circle was found on an ancient stone, it predates Christianity and later became a common Celtic symbol for the life of the Christian Trinity. It is a fitting symbol for Woman, who spiral out with constant concern as the carers for all humanity and spiral-in attending to themselves with respect and love. Two spirals are firmly poised on the earth and the third is aspiring up to a spiritual transcendence. However, the spiral is a positive symbol that belongs to everyone and excludes no one. It is the journey of life that calls for the voice of all God's creation to be heard in a Trinitarian non- hierarchical world of justice. For CWO it is particularly a clarion call for the end of the 'sin of sexism 'against women historically embedded in the RC Church.

Origin of the Logo for CWO was the work of
Veronica Seddon and Lala Winkley.

Lightning Source UK Ltd.
Milton Keynes UK
UKOW06f0953311215

265616UK00001B/39/P